Judgment Detox

Release the Beliefs That Hold You Back from Living a Better Life

Gabrielle Bernstein

NORTH STAR WAY

New York   London   Toronto   Sydney   New Delhi

NORTH
STAR
WAY

North Star Way
An Imprint of Simon & Schuster, Inc.
1230 Avenue of the Americas
New York, NY 10020

First North Star Way hardcover edition January 2018

NORTH STAR WAY and colophon are trademarks of
Simon & Schuster, Inc.

For information about special discounts for bulk purchases, please
contact Simon & Schuster Special Sales at 1-866-506-1949 or
business@simonandschuster.com.

The North Star Way Speakers Bureau can bring authors to your
live event. For more information or to book an event, contact
the North Star Way Speakers Bureau at 1-212-698-8888 or visit
our website at www.thenorthstarway.com.

Interior design by Bryden Spevak

Manufactured in the United States of America

10 9 8 7 6 5 4 3 2 1

Library of Congress Cataloging-in-Publication Data

Names: Bernstein, Gabrielle, author.
Title: Judgment detox : release the beliefs that hold you back from living a
better life / Gabrielle Bernstein.
Description: New York : North Star Way, 2018.
Identifiers: LCCN 2017021778| ISBN 9781501168963 (hardback) | ISBN
9781501168994 (ebook)
Subjects: LCSH: Self-actualization (Psychology) | Judgment. | Happiness. |
   BISAC: SELF-HELP / Personal Growth / Happiness. | SELF-HELP /
Motivational
   & Inspirational. | BODY, MIND & SPIRIT / Inspiration & Personal Growth.
Classification: LCC BF637.S4 B4747 2018 | DDC 158—dc23 LC record available
at https://lccn.loc.gov/2017021778

ISBN 978-1-5011-6896-3
ISBN 978-1-5011-6899-4 (ebook)

CONTENTS

Judgment Detox

The Judgment Detox

My fingers are trembling as I begin this introduction. I have a limiting belief on repeat: *Who are you to write a book called* Judgment Detox? *You judge all the time!*

I take a deep breath and pull myself together. I have a book deal, a deadline, and a commitment. I've got to write this book.

I sit in stillness with my hands on the keyboard. I take a deep breath and continue typing.

YOUR TRUTH IS WHAT HEALS

I sigh with relief and accept that the more honest and authentic I am about my own struggles with judgment, the better this book will be. I accept that my suffering is yours. No matter how spiritual, kind, or compassionate we may be, we all suffer from judgment. Judgment is all-pervasive.

My commitment as a spiritual teacher is to keep it real. In order for this relationship to work I have to tell you the truth.

So here goes:

I struggle with judgment every day. I judge far and I judge wide. I judge strangers for divergent political views. I judge acquaintances on social media for the comments they make. I judge the way people discipline their children. I judge the girl moving too slowly in the line ahead of me. I judge my husband for not responding to me exactly how I want him to respond. And of course I judge myself for just about everything.

For years I tried to justify or rationalize or dismiss what seemed like innocent enough behavior. We get a quick hit of self-righteousness when we judge others. It's a reliable little crutch when we feel hurt, insecure, or vulnerable. Our judgments toward others seem to make us feel better than them—smarter, savvier, more enlightened, healthier, or wealthier.

Inevitably, though, this feeling fades. When I judge, I feel my energy weaken and my thoughts darken. Time and time again, judgment left me feeling deeply uncomfortable, isolated, and out of alignment with the woman I want to be.

My definition of judgment for this book is pretty straightforward: separation from love. The moment we see ourselves as separate from anyone else, we detour into a false belief system that is out of alignment with our true nature, which is love. Deep down we are all loving, kind, and compassionate beings. There are many spiritual terms for this truth, such as *Buddha nature, spirit, source,* and *God.* Throughout the book I'll refer to this truthful state as *love.* This separation from love is the force behind everything from playground bullying to systemic racism, xenophobic world leaders, and even terrorism. We are living in divisive times, and separation has become the norm. When we feel attacked by someone, our response is to attack back. We feel justified in fighting back and defending ourselves from attack. Of course this only creates more separation, compounding the problem. The Internet, unfortunately, can exacerbate this issue. We see people of all ages cyberbullying others via social media with devastating consequences. There are so many stories of high school and college students committing suicide over negative posts and harassment, and even more cases of otherwise happy people finding themselves depressed after comparing their lives to the curated galleries on photo-sharing apps.

For more than a decade as a spiritual student and teacher, I've committed to taking an honest inventory of my fear, judgment, and separation. Through my willingness and honesty I've been able to heal my struggles with judgment. Throughout this book I will tell you the truth about my suffering and I'll share the lessons that have benefitted me. These are lessons that I practice daily, and which have given me great relief. While I still struggle with judgment, I've experienced a miraculous shift. Let me be clear: The miracle is not that I've rid myself of all judgmental thoughts. The miracle is that I no longer believe in them. So while the habit of judgment continues to challenge me, through my spiritual practice I've come to accept that judgment is not who I am.

To begin the journey of healing judgment and restoring love, we must recognize that we all have the same problem and the same solution. Our problem is that we separated from love and the solution is to return to love.

Let's try to understand why we separated from love in the first place. From a spiritual perspective, our life's hang-ups stem from this moment of separation, when our internal voice of fear (our ego) led us astray from love, compassion, and oneness. Our separation from love can be the result of a deeply traumatic experience or a seemingly insignificant event. Regardless of the trigger, however, it first happens the moment we come to see ourselves as separate from others or not good enough in some way.

The separation from love can begin as early as infancy. Babies can be born into a hostile environment that leaves them neglected and with the belief that they are unprotected in an unsafe world. Or the separation can come the moment children notice they are being treated differently because of their race or religion or gender. In that instant their sense of oneness is taken from them, and they learn to see the divisiveness of the world.

At some point in our childhood, most of us are told we're not smart enough, strong enough, or pretty enough, or that we lack some other positive quality. We then start to see ourselves as apart from others. This separation makes us feel alone in the world.

The separation can also spawn from the desire to feel special or "better than." For instance, a child who grows up witnessing the consequences of privilege may come to believe the false notion that people with money are special.

While we all have different stories that caused us to separate from love, we all have the same response to feeling alone in the world: fear. Separating from love is a traumatic event, and when we're traumatized, we feel unsafe. One way we respond to that feeling of fear is to fight back through attacking and judging of others. It's an attempt to build ourselves up and lean on judgment as our great protector.

The ego voice of fear thrives on the belief that we are separate. The metaphysical text *A Course in Miracles* teaches that the ego reinforces our separation by convincing us that we're less special or more special than others. *Special* implies that someone is better than you because they have more— earn more money or are more attractive or accomplished or famous or are of the "right" race or religion. It works the same in the other direction too, where you make yourself special in the face of another's perceived lack of something. When we see the world through the lens of specialness, the dark cloud of judgment blocks us from our light and connection to others.

One manifestation of specialness is the *special relationship,* which the ego uses to protect us from feeling the pain of separation. We feel a tremendous amount of guilt and a deeply uncomfortable sense of incompleteness as a result of separating from love and cutting off our truth. We try to find relief in someone else, choosing to believe that another person can "complete" us and projecting our guilt onto them. This is how the special relationship is created.

The special relationship presents itself in many areas of our lives. For instance, maybe you've made your teachers or mentors special because you look up to them and they've guided you through a unique time in your life. Or maybe you've turned a romantic partner into an idol, feeling like you can't survive without his or her love and attention. Special relationships can sometimes appear harmless, like the specialness you project onto a parent. This one can seem counterintuitive because while your family members may have greatly supported your growth and provided you with a source of inspiration, they're not your saviors.

Whomever you've made special will inevitably disappoint you in some way. Their ego will always shine through (they are human, after all) and you'll be left frustrated and feeling alone. This experience reinforces the devastation of the initial feelings of separation. In response to this desolation, you'll judge the special person for not being who you thought (or hoped) they were. When your idol falls, you fall with them. Whenever we believe anyone to be the source of our happiness or pain, we ultimately project our guilt onto them and begin the judgment cycle.

THE JUDGMENT CYCLE

Our true nature is love. But at some point in our life, usually in childhood, some external event causes us to separate from that true nature. That separation from love creates in us feelings of specialness or inadequacy, leading to loneliness, and as a result, fear. We want to protect ourselves from that fear, so we project it outward in the form of judgment.

We know we are loving, interconnected beings, but in our separation we live in a dream state, shutting off our connection to our loving truth. This separation establishes the ego's perception of a false *self* based on judgment. We grow to believe deeply in the false perception of ourselves in order to feel safe in the world of separation.

Deep down, and without realizing it, we judge ourselves for separating from our truth, leading us to feel ashamed and guilty. That unconscious guilt is so painful that we have no choice but to project it outward in an effort to end our suffering. By projecting judgment onto others, we deny and repress our feelings of guilt. Subconsciously this makes us feel even *more* guilty because we know this judgment is not who we really are. The guilt we feel from judging others is then projected right back onto ourselves, and the vicious cycle begins again. This is the judgment cycle.

I cannot overstate this: Judgment is the number one reason we feel blocked, sad, and alone. Our popular culture and media place enormous value on social status, looks, racial and religious separation, and material wealth. We are made to feel less than, separate, and not good enough, so we use judgment to insulate ourselves from the pain of feeling inadequate, insecure, or unworthy. It's easier to make fun of, write off, or judge someone for a perceived weakness of theirs than it is to examine our own sense of lack.

JUDGMENT IS AN ADDICTIVE PATTERN

Judgment is an addiction response to deep-rooted trauma. The first trauma is the separation from love. From a spiritual perspective, choosing fear and separation over love dissociates us from our truth. We become fragmented in this state of separation and lose our connection to our inner being. In this disconnected state, we inadvertently turn our back on our inner being and become obsessed with an outward projection of who we think we are. Feelings of guilt and sadness wash over us, because deep down, we know we've turned our back on love. But we can't fully understand our guilt, so we do whatever we can to avoid feeling it. This is how the cycle of judgment becomes an addictive pattern.

When we avoid our guilt and suffering by projecting it onto others, it's a way of numbing out. Like any good drug, judgment will anesthetize our pain and redirect our focus. It can even get us high. Gossip is a great example. Whenever you get together with friends to talk about another person in a judgmental way, you're avoiding your own core wounds. You're using judgment as a drug to numb your own pain and get high on someone else's. Gossip is especially nasty because it gives us the illusion that we're bonding with others, when instead we're just banding together to heap all our pain onto another person.

Gossiping can give us a buzz because it provides temporary relief from self-judgment and attack. We repeat a self-judgmental story on a loop all day long: *I'm not good enough. Why did I make that mistake? I'm ugly. I'm not smart enough.* And so on. All these self-inflicted behaviors are just another form of addiction. We unconsciously choose to judge rather than feel the pain beneath our wounds.

But notice I said that our self-judgmental story is played on a loop. That's because it leads nowhere! Getting on the path to healing requires us to feel the discomfort—but we're way too scared to go there, so instead we gossip or judge ourselves. We perceive ourselves as the victim of the world we see. Judging ourselves as the victim feels safer than facing our wounds. This is how self-judgment becomes an addiction.

The addictive pattern is further fueled by our denial. We long to feel better but deny that judgment is the problem. In fact, we see judgment as the solution, as a way of protecting ourselves. Our unconscious belief system keeps us stuck in the judgment cycle because we're terrified of facing our own pain and suffering. We use judgment to protect ourselves from exposing our deepest wounds.

The repetition of judgment is habit-forming. If you repeat a behavior over and over, you strengthen your neural pathways. In time that behavior becomes second nature. The more you repeat the pattern of judgment, the more you believe in it. The metaphysical teachers Abraham-Hicks say, "A belief is just a thought you keep thinking." You create your reality with the thoughts you repeat and the beliefs that you align with. When judgment is your belief system, you'll always feel unsafe, under attack, and defensive. If you're going to change the habit of judgment you need to change your core belief system. Our aim is to find our way back home—to find our way back to love.

THE PATHWAY TO HEALING JUDGMENT

From the moment of separation we've been living in a bad dream, and the habit of judgment has kept us asleep. Healing judgment is the undoing of the dream and the return to peace.

When I became more conscious of my own judgmental nature, I began to feel myself wake up. I lovingly witnessed my behavior and noticed that seemingly innocent and minor moments of judgment were just as destructive as outward negativity and attack. I could no longer ignore the guilt I felt from being stuck in the judgment cycle. Instead of pushing through it, ignoring the behavior or choosing to deal with it later, I decided to face it head on.

Therefore I set out to heal myself from the judgment cycle. I knew that if I was serious about ending the cycle, I'd have to accept the solution, even if it meant changing a belief system I'd lived by for decades. So I put myself through a process of personal growth and spiritual development, exploring transformational practices to heal my perception of judgment for good.

This is a process of undoing the belief system of judgment that has caused much suffering so that we can return to peace. Through my personal healing journey I created the six steps you will find in this book. I've put myself through all six steps and continue to practice them daily.

By fearlessly committing to this Judgment Detox, here's what I've learned:

First, I learned that we don't have to give up judgment altogether. In many cases we need it. We need to discern what feels safe and what doesn't. We must honor what feels right to us morally. Also, this practice doesn't necessarily affect certain kinds of judgments, such as what to eat, who to date, or which model of car to drive. In fact, it's more useful to think of these acts as discernments or personal choices. We can use logic and intuition to discern what feels right for us without being judgmental. It's the habit of condemning and criticizing that we must let go of. One way you know you're in judgment (and not discernment) is that you don't feel good; instead you feel defensive, fearful, or under attack. It's a sign you've separated from love and chosen fear. When you make a decision that feels good and flows from your authentic truth, you know it's not backed with the ego's judgment.

Second, I learned that when we judge others, we're really judging a disowned part of our own shadow. Whatever we resent or dislike in another person is a reflection of something we dislike in ourselves or a representation of a deep wound we're unwilling to heal. Often other people trigger our wounds. We judge them when this happens instead of accepting that the discomfort is really about us.

Third, I learned that judgment may give you a high at first, but it results in a hangover that really sucks. Judgment lowers our energy and weakens us physically and mentally. It makes us feel alone and cut off from inspiration and love.

Finally, I discovered that as thorny and difficult as judgment may be, loosening judgment's grip is pretty simple: Look at all the fear and bring it to the light. By bringing your judgment to the light through the practices in this book, you'll begin to have a new relationship to it. Like any great detox, you flush out toxins so that you feel healthier. In your newly clear state, you become aware of how the habit hurts you and you intuitively know how to handle it.

My commitment to healing my own relationship to judgment has changed my life in profound ways. My awareness of my judgment has helped me become a more mindful and conscious person. My willingness to revise these perceptions has set me free. I have been able to let go of resentments and jealousies, I can face pain with curiosity and love, and I forgive others and myself much more easily. Best of all, I have a healthy relationship to judgment so that I can witness when it shows up and can use these steps to quickly return to love.

The Judgment Detox is an interactive six-step process that calls on spiritual principles from the text *A Course in Miracles*, Kundalini yoga, the Emotional Freedom Techniques (also known as tapping), meditation, prayer, and other metaphysical teachings. I've demystified these principles to make them easy to commit to and apply in your daily life. Each lesson builds upon the next to support true healing. When you follow the process and become willing to let go, judgment, pain, and suffering will begin to dissolve.

Before we dive into the rest of the book and start detoxing, I want to give you a short overview of each step so you know what's coming. Here's how it all works.

Step 1: Witness Your Judgment Without Judgment

When I started to witness how my judgmental nature made me feel, right away I could see why my life wasn't flowing. Judgment made me feel weak, sad, and disconnected. It even caused me physical pain. Once I was able to step away from the judgment and witness how it made me feel, I could truly understand how much it was blocking my happiness.

In most cases we don't even realize how judgmental we are. This is partly because we judge ourselves for our judgmental behavior. It sounds crazy, but we do it all the time. We can be tempted to criticize ourselves for our judgment or to feel shame for our thoughts or behavior. Instead, when we take an honest inventory, we must honor ourselves for having the willingness to look with love at whatever judgmental choices we've made. The way out of judgment begins when you witness the judgment *without more judgment*. When we look at our judgment with love, we can begin the healing process.

In Step 1 you'll get intimate with your judgment, identify the triggers underneath it, and get honest about how it makes you feel. You'll be guided to uncover the stories from your past that spark your judgmental behavior, and you'll come to understand how all judgment is a disowned part of your own shadow. This authentic audit of your behavior is a necessary first step. Without it, you can't move on to the next phase of healing. The spiritual path to clearing judgment begins with your honest inventory.

Step 2: Honor the Wound

The next step in healing your relationship to judgment is to honor the shadows and bring them to the light. In this step I teach a powerful technique called the Emotional Freedom Techniques, also known as EFT, or tapping. EFT is a psychological acupressure technique that supports your emotional health. I have found EFT to be one of the greatest ways to address the root cause of emotional issues that live below the surface of our judgment.

The practice of EFT asks that you tap on specific energy meridians on your body. When these meridians are stimulated, they tell the amygdala (the part of our brain that triggers the fight/flight/freeze response) to calm down. When the amygdala gets the message that it's safe to relax, a major shift can occur in your emotional state. I have created specific scripts to address many of our most common trigger issues. As you tap on the specific meridians you'll be guided to address certain emotions that come up around your stress. This practice will help you heal the triggers, wounds, and traumas that live beneath your judgments. This process alone can have a huge healing effect on your life. I teach EFT in the second step of the Judgment Detox so you can feel significant relief from the get-go.

Step 3: Put Love on the Altar

Once you've witnessed your judgmental thoughts and honored the wounds through EFT, we pray. This is a practice of offering up your judgment through prayer. An essential part of this work is establishing a relationship to a power greater than you (however you might define it). Through the spiritual practice of surrender, you begin to dissolve judgment with love.

Some judgments are harder than others to let go of. Some may feel especially difficult or even impossible. This is where the power of prayer comes in. You don't have to rely entirely on yourself; instead, you can call on a power greater than you for guidance and support. Offering up your judgment through prayer lifts the burden from your shoulders while signaling to the Universe that you are willing to see a person or situation differently, even if you're not sure how to do it.

Prayer offers you a shift in perception, which will in turn help you see your judgments through the lens of love and compassion. If you have a hard time finding things you like about a person or a situation, you can call on compassion. When you cultivate a feeling of compassion, judgment cannot coexist. Compassion is the antidote to judgment. Instead of perceiving someone's behavior or a situation as a threat, you can witness it as a call for love.

Finally, in Step 3 you take time to be compassionate toward yourself. Judgment wouldn't be present if in some way you weren't calling out for love.

Step 4: See for the First Time

Once you've prayed and cultivated compassion, you'll be ready to shift how you see the people you've judged. We often judge others (and ourselves) by projecting old experiences onto our current circumstances. But when you practice seeing someone for the first time, you release them from the false projections you've put on them and the false beliefs that separate you. Instead of seeing another person through the lens of the past, you'll see them as someone calling out for love.

We begin to heal our judgment toward others when we accept that people are our teachers in the classroom that is our life. Making that commitment lets us look at our situation differently. You'll witness how you drag the past into the present, and then you'll be able to choose again. You'll learn how you can choose to look at a person (or a situation) as if you're seeing them for the first time. Imagine how free you would be if you didn't lug your past into your present with every encounter! Remember that we are all caught in the same cycle of fear and are all desperately seeking a way out. The way out is through love.

Step 5: Cut the Cords

Learning how to see others for the first time sets you up for the powerful practice of meditation. Some of my greatest healing has occurred on my meditation pillow—because in stillness all separation melts away and oneness is restored. Step 5 contains visualization meditations, Kundalini meditations, and mantra-based meditations to help you heal your relationship to judgment. There are six meditations. Practice one a day for six days in the order in which they are presented. Each meditation builds upon the next, helping you relinquish attack thoughts and reconnect to your inner guidance system. Following each meditation you'll be asked to free-write in your journal. This free-writing process will allow your inner wisdom to come to the forefront and reveal whatever you need to know for deeper healing and growth. You'll be amazed by what comes through!

After practicing the six meditations, I suggest you choose a favorite and make it a daily practice. These meditations will help you experience great relief and stay consistent with your Judgment Detox.

Step 6: Bring Your Shadows to Light

The final step of the Judgment Detox is to let yourself off the hook for the judgments you have made. This is possible when you understand that when you judge, you're really just looking for love. It's the true intent behind the attack. Deep down all you want is to protect yourself from not feeling loved. It's also the intent of the person you believe has attacked *you*. We're all simply looking for love.

In fact, attack, fear, judgment, and any form of separation are all just calls for help. When you're in physical pain, you *know* that your pain calls for relief. The same is true for judgment. It's a form of emotional pain that you want to relieve. You do not want to remain sick, sad, or fearful. In any given moment that you witness yourself in judgment, you can set yourself free by simply forgiving the thought. Forgive yourself for having the thought and even forgive the thought itself.

You want to be free. When you witness your judgment without judgment, accept that you have chosen fear, and remain open to receiving the help you're calling for. You can liberate yourself from this pattern.

The Judgment Detox dissolves all boundaries with love. It brings us back to this truth: We're all in it together. We all suffer. We all feel unworthy and abandoned. But identifying sameness in one another allows us to shift our focus from separation back to love. We share the thought system of fear and we share the loving mind. We share the same capacity to choose love over fear. As my dear teacher Kenneth Wapnick said, "We see that we all have the same interest of awakening from the dream of unkindness and returning to the kindness who created us kind."

A WORLD BEYOND JUDGMENT

If you're ready to begin the journey of undoing the false perception of separation and specialness, then get psyched for what's to come! This book offers a path to undo the pattern of judgment to return to oneness, peace, and inner harmony.

There are a few things to consider, however, before embarking on this detox. First, I recommend that you stay consistent. Like any detox, the more committed you are, the greater the results will be. I also recommend that you document your progress along the way. Don't be afraid to celebrate your moments of success. This is an important part of the process, because the healthier you become, the more your ego will resist your growth. Therefore, consciously creating space to celebrate your shifts will help you avoid judging your practice.

It's also important to pay attention to the ways your ego will sneak in. Whenever we shine light on the darkness, the ego works overtime. I want to call out your ego's resistance now so that you're ready for it when it sneaks up on you. The ego will deny your recovery and judge your results. Throughout the book I'll ask you to look closely at how you've contributed to your own suffering and pain. You'll be challenged to see your shadows and witness your negative patterns. When you do this, your self-judgment will be triggered. In a space of self-judgment we can get paralyzed with fear and may want to stop. Be aware of this now so you can identify your ego's resistance when it shows up. Every person reading this book will fall into the trap of self-judgment along the way. I felt it throughout the entire writing process! The deeper I went into each step, the louder my inner critic became. But instead of succumbing to the voice of fear, I surrendered to the love that lives within each step. The best way to combat the voice of self-judgment is to dive deeper into the practices of the Judgment Detox. Each step will offer you new layers of relief and freedom. Trust the process and stay consistent.

THE PROMISE OF HEALING JUDGMENT

This six-step practice offers many promises. Petty resentments will disappear, compassion will replace attack, the energy of resistance will transform into freedom, and you'll feel more peace and happiness than you've ever known. I can testify to these results because I've lived them. I've never felt more freedom and joy than I have when writing and practicing these steps.

And the miracles keep coming. Once you begin to feel better, you start to release your resistance to love. The more you practice these steps, the more love enters into your consciousness and into your energetic vibration. When you're in harmony with love, you receive more of what you want. Your energy attracts its likeness. So when you shift your energy from defensive judgment to free-flowing love, your life gets awesome. You'll attract exactly what you need, your relationships will heal, your health will improve, and you'll feel safer and more secure.

I wrote this book to help us all feel better. As a spiritual activist I believe that my greatest contribution to the world is to help people reconnect to the power of love. When we make this shift, we begin to vibrate at a new frequency. When you change your frequency, your family, neighbors, and friends reap the benefits. One person's energetic shift has the power to create a ripple effect across the globe. And as more and more people vibrate love, the vibrations of hate and judgment weaken. The times we're living in require our commitment to love. We are divided, fearful, angry, and traumatized. The only way to survive these times is to change our frequency. This practice is not just about feeling happier and attracting more—it's about healing the world.

We all feel the call of our own inner activist. The most powerful way to respond to that call is to shift our inner life. When we make inner shifts, we intuitively know how to show up on the outside. We lead from a place of compassion and forgiveness. We become more conscious on our social media feed and in our face-to-face conversations. We become a better example for our children. And each loving thought we have becomes a peaceful protest that energetically heals the epidemic of hate in the world. One loving thought at a time creates a miracle. Follow these steps to clear all blocks, spread more love, and live a miraculous life.

IMPORTANT RESOURCES FOR SUPPORT

There are several additional resources I've created and gathered to support you on your path. Throughout the book I'll reference these, which you can find at GabbyBernstein.com/JudgmentDetox. Each step requires journaling exercises

that you can do in your favorite notebook or in the Judgment Detox journal. The Judgment Detox journal is designed specifically for you to celebrate the miracles and document your process every step of the way. On the Resources page (GabbyBernstein.com/bookresources), you'll also find other guided materials that will support your journey!

Let's get started. Flip the page and begin Step 1 of the Judgment Detox.

Witness Your Judgment Without Judgment

It's the morning of November 9, 2016. The election results are in and the nation is divided. The country is polarized and overwhelmed by the divisive campaigning. Both political parties are exhausted by the drama, the negative rhetoric, and the judgment. Half the country is celebrating the results while the other half is protesting in the streets.

It's early in the morning and I turn on the news. Every station is swamped with political pundits spewing conflicting views. I turn to Facebook only to find nasty, heated debates taking over my feed. I'm saddened by the energy of separation and the attack from both sides. Moments later I get a text from my publicist saying, "Gab, I've got a ton of online publications that want you to come on today and share your spiritual response to the election and the division between both parties." Without hesitation I text back: "Yes!"

After accepting the media requests, I come to the realization that I haven't yet found my own spiritual solution to handling the conflict in our country. I take a good look at where I'm at: deeply disturbed by the negativity I'm witnessing all throughout the US. How can I offer spiritual guidance in the midst of such immense separation? Despite my apprehension I feel I have no choice but to show up. I have to call on my higher self to shine some light on the darkness.

Within the hour I'm on Livestream sharing spiritual guidance on how to respond to the election. The interviewer says, "Gabby, the nation is divided and we need your help. What is the spiritual way to handle this?" Before I respond, I silently pray, "Spirit, please speak through me." Then I start with my truth. I share how overwhelmed I feel by all of it. Then these words pour out of me effortlessly: "We must look closely at our shadow and shine light on it. Let's all take a look at our judgment. Let's become aware of the ways that we've judged the president-elect, his team, his family, and his supporters. Let's look at the ways we judged Hillary Clinton and her family and her campaign. Let's get honest about how we've judged our friends, neighbors, and families for their conflicting political views. The first step in healing our feelings of separateness is to witness our judgment without judgment. The one thing we all have in common is our judgment. It's all the same, regardless of which side we're on."

The interviewer seems surprised my response. She, like many, felt justified in her judgment.

"What do I do with my judgment?" she asks.

"Just witness it and trust that this is the first step toward healing," I say. I explain that in order to truly heal our feelings of judgment, we must begin by healing our minds. We must acknowledge that attacking someone who has attacked us only creates more attack. If we want to free ourselves from this nasty cycle, we have to shine light on the darkness. The way to do this is to witness our judgmental thoughts.

When I suggest that we simply witness our judgment and trust in the healing power of this action, I can sense relief in my interviewer's voice and expression. When we let our guard down and witness our judgment with love even for a moment, we can experience peace.

Being the nonjudgmental witness of your judgment is the first step in this detox. This is the crux of the work. We have to see clearly the ways in which we separate from love, and we have to get honest about the dark corners of our mind. The crucial part of this practice is to witness our judgment *without judgment.*

The process of witnessing our darkness is a brave and sacred act of love. Being willing to accept the parts of our consciousness that are out of spiritual alignment makes us stronger.

When we take an honest inventory of the ways we judge, we can become aware of the root cause of all our suffering: our separation from love. At our core we are loving, kind, whole, healthy, and compassionate people. But over the course of our lives we've separated from that love and wholeness. We've become fragmented beings with dark, scary parts. Rage, anger, trauma, and painful memories contribute to a sense of dissociation. We become numb, frozen, and asleep. We shut down the power of our love and innocence in an attempt to protect ourselves from feeling our deepest, most shameful wounds. We've done the best we can to survive, and we've grown to rely on attack and fear the presence of love.

In many cases, judgment has been our greatest defense mechanism. We have used it to defend against our vulnerability. We fear that if we let our guard down and act compassionately and lovingly toward one another that we will be taken advantage of and will no longer be safe. This is totally understandable given the traumas we've experienced in the past and all the new traumatic events in the world. All we have to do is turn on the news and we're engulfed in the negativity of it all. So day after day, month after month, year after year we've built up a wall against the presence of love and instead grown to rely on judgment as our protector.

Behind the wall of judgment lie our deepest feelings of inadequacy and shame. When we feel separate from others, our shame is triggered. We feel alone, not good enough— unworthy of love and connection. Shame is the most difficult emotion to accept, and we'll do anything to avoid feeling it. We resist it by projecting it onto others through judgment, and then we grow to rely on judgment as a way of finding relief from our wounds.

The first step in healing our shame and letting down our guard is to accept that we are not the victim of the world we see. By witnessing our judgment with love and compassion for ourselves, we can see how our wounded side is trying to protect us from feeling shame. But this is a false protection. The more conscious we become of how we use judgment to "play it safe," the more we realize how unsafe it really is. We can begin to see how judgment breeds more judgment. When we attempt to protect ourselves with judgment, we create more separation and deepen our disconnection from love. Love can seem far scarier to us than fear. We're terri-fied to let love in, because we fear that when we do, we'll be susceptible to more pain.

But love is the antidote to judgment. Love heals it all.

When we witness our judgment with love, we can see ourselves as innocent children. We can see our wounds and begin to understand why we would judge in the first place. If you have been abused as a child, of course you would judge the world around you because you don't feel safe. If you have been left by a lover, it's inevitable that you'd judge all future relationships to protect yourself from being hurt again. If you've felt bullied or attacked, of course you would attack back to try to save yourself from pain and suffering.

Today in my country, following our presidential elec-tion, I'm witnessing millions of people's childhood wounds triggered beyond all measure. They feel left behind and ig-nored. They feel bullied. They feel sexually assaulted. They feel like targets of bigotry. Their wounds have been ripped open, and their instinct to protect themselves has kicked in with a fierceness.

I honor their feelings. At the same time, I witness their wounds. I can see clearly how their judgment is a defense mechanism. I can also see how we all hold so tightly to our own defenses. To release our judgments of one another would be to take off our armor and end the fight. Traumatized people cannot let their guard down. But what would happen if everyone raging on every side took a moment to witness their judgment? They'd realize that *at its core,* their judgment is no different from anyone else's. Their fear is the same. Their wound is the same.

WE ARE ALL WOUNDED

We are all innocent children who became deeply traumatized. We are afraid of love and we use judgment to protect ourselves. In many cases separation and judgment represent the only way we could survive. Honoring the ways we've stayed safe is a huge step.

Our judgment of others has protected us from facing our wounds. To avoid feeling our wounds we've built up pretenses around ourselves. We mask our wounds underneath our clothes, in our relationships, and behind our social and economic status. The perceptions we've built up around ourselves are like blinding lights we shine to distract from the shadows within. We rely on them because without them our vulnerability would be exposed.

We put enormous effort into hiding our vulnerability, but it's our vulnerability that truly heals. When we feel safe enough to expose our shadows, that's when we become free. We don't have to protect our shadows any longer. We can begin to dismantle the wall that separates us from real, authentic, fearless love. By witnessing our judgment we take down the first brick in the wall and peek at what's behind it—our shame, fear, and feelings of separation. Uncovering our true feelings helps us understand our triggers and honor our wounds so that we can work through them. When we witness our judgment we accept that it was merely a defense against our wounds.

This brings us to the first step in the Judgment Detox.

WITNESS YOUR JUDGMENT WITHOUT JUDGMENT

This is a beautiful practice. What is asked is that you become more conscious of the ways you separate yourself from others and the world. This step requires an honest inventory of your thoughts, words, and actions. When you look closely at the ways you judge, you may be tempted to judge yourself. Let's take that off the table now by accepting that *we all judge all the time!* We live in a world filled with judgment and no one is a saint. Therefore, let's accept that we're all in it together. I know that makes me feel better.

Whenever I judge myself for judging, I try to remember that I'm not alone. I remember that judgment is a pervasive addiction. When I witness my judgment without judgment

I can be proud of my willingness to heal and grow. I can applaud myself for stepping out of the darkness and turning on the light. I honor myself for the traumas that led me to be so defensive in the first place. After all, why would I feel the need to judge if I felt safe and complete? It's the dark beliefs within me that lead me to judge. I use judgment to take the focus off my own feelings of inadequacy and I project those feelings onto someone else to feel relief. But instead of bringing me the relief I desire, projecting my judgment onto others severs my connection with my truth. After the projection, I'm left feeling disconnected, fearful, and alone. I feel separate from others and unsafe in my perception of the world. The aftermath of judgment is a dark and scary place that offers me no relief.

Real relief comes when I am brave enough to witness the judgment and call it by its name: fear. The root cause of all judgment is the fear of not being good enough, not being worthy of love, and not being safe. When we become brave enough to look at the judgment and fear, we can begin to heal.

I've made a major commitment as a spiritual teacher to show up for the world with love and grace. This doesn't come easily to me. I often feel wounded, offended, and defensive. But in order to show up for my readers and for myself I've become a master at witnessing my judgment.

This step in the Judgment Detox is the most crucial of

the practice. Without your honesty and willingness to look at the darkness you can never step into the light.

TAKE THE FIRST STEP INTO THE LIGHT

The spiritual teacher and author Eckhart Tolle says, "The moment you become aware of the ego in you, it is strictly speaking no longer the ego, but just an old, conditioned mind-pattern. Ego implies unawareness. Awareness and ego cannot coexist."

The first step in the Judgment Detox is a process of becoming aware of the dark shadows in your mind. When you become aware of your darkness, a profound shift occurs—and you no longer have to run from fear. When you expose your fear to the light, suddenly there's nothing to run from. You can see the fear as something outside of you, something you no longer need to identify with. You can witness the fear and judgment as an addictive pattern rather than a personality trait. Witnessing strips fear and judgment of their power and liberates you.

As you can probably guess, being present with your fear can feel terrifying. You may be afraid of exposing the darkness because you're scared of what may be lurking below the surface. That's why the Judgment Detox is a step-by-step process. You won't expose the darkness to the light all at once. You begin by witnessing what's present right now so that bit by bit, piece by piece, you can become more and more aware. This process is meant to be taken slowly so that you can truly witness your judgmental patterns. All that's required right now is your willingness to begin the journey of healing your mind so you can be free.

Are you willing to look at your judgment and bring awareness to it?

I trust the answer is yes. Without your willingness you wouldn't have picked up this book. Your desire to be free, happy, and connected is what led you here. So let's call on that willingness with a prayer and allow you to look at your judgment without fear or self-attack. Prayer is a key element to true spiritual healing. When you pray, you offer up your fearful beliefs to the care of your loving inner guidance system. A prayer can disconnect you from the habit of fear and judgment so that you can open up your consciousness to hear the voice of love.

This prayer will help you surrender to the spiritual steps laid out before you. Allow it to guide you to commit to your desire to be free and to begin Step 1.

Let's pray:

I thank my higher self, the voice of love and
wisdom within me. Thank you for granting me

the willingness to open this book and begin this journey. I am willing to be free. I am willing to be happy. I am willing to witness my judgment without judgment.

Now that you're energetically prepared to look at your judgment, take out your notebook and pen.

At the top of the page write this: *I am willing to witness my judgment without judgment.*

Then make four columns down the page. If you want to follow this practice with the Judgment Detox journal, the columns will be laid out for you. To access the journal visit GabbyBernstein.com/bookresources.

Column 1: What or whom am I judging?

Column 2: How does this judgment make me feel?

Column 3: Why do I feel justified in this judgment?

Column 4: What moment in my life triggered me to feel justified in this judgment?

Here are two examples of how to use the four-column process:

What or whom am I judging?	How does this judgment make me feel?	Why do I feel justified in this judgment?	What moment in my life triggered me to feel justified in this judgment?
I'm judging know-it-all academics for thinking they're better than everyone else.	It makes me feel good at first because I feel like I'm protecting myself from people who think they are better than me. But when I sit with my feelings, I feel separate and alone.	Because academics are know-it-alls and they think they're better than anyone who doesn't have their vocabulary and knowledge.	When I was in sixth grade the smart, popular boy I had a crush on told me I was stupid.
I judge my best friend for dating guys who are not good for her.	I feel justified at first, but quickly that turns into sadness and even jealousy.	I think she's better than the guys she dates. She deserves more.	This judgment is triggered by the fact that I don't choose guys that are good for me. In fact, I don't even date because I'm too afraid of being hurt. This all stems from the traumatic breakup I had last year.

Begin with column 1. List whatever comes to mind. Don't edit yourself at all—just write out every judgment that comes up. Try to make a list of at least fifteen judgments (sticking *only* to column 1 for each). You can start with a minor judgment if it feels too scary to throw out the big ones first. Maybe you judged a stranger in line at the grocery store because of what she was wearing. Maybe you judged a Facebook friend for one of her posts. There are many small judgments we make throughout the day. The more you allow yourself to become aware of them, the more obvious they will be. Don't discredit the seemingly minor judgments because you may discover a bigger pattern at work.

Once you've written out fifteen judgments, take a moment to review the list *without editing it*. You may find that some of the judgments you recorded don't feel very heightened for you at this time. Keep them on the list nonetheless. Trust that whatever you put on the page is exposing something to you. Even if it seems like a minor judgment, there's something underneath it that needs to be exposed. Trust completely in what you've written.

Once you've documented at least fifteen judgments, move on to column 2. This is where you get honest about how judgment makes you feel. We don't often take a step back from our attack thoughts and check in with the feelings underneath them. In fact, this may be the first time you've even considered it. I understand that this might feel pretty uncomfortable and foreign. But please don't skip this step! It's crucial that you become intimate with the feelings behind your judgment. Those feelings will help inform what comes next.

Go down the list of judgments and describe in great detail how each one makes you feel. Be very descriptive. Maybe you feel like you're choking, or that the judgment makes you feel like you want to punch a wall. Or maybe the judgment makes you feel justified, empowered, and fierce. I recommend that you go as far as describing how it feels in your body. Where do you hold this judgment in your physical being? Does the judgment have a color or a shape? Does it cause you physical tension or pain? Does it make your skin tingle or your chest tighten? Vividly describe how the judgment makes you feel.

When you've completed column 2, fill in column 3. Take time to write out all the reasons you feel justified in your judgment. *Do not judge your justification or feel guilty about or ashamed of your thoughts.* Rather, give yourself full permission to get it out onto the page. Honor it. This is a process of stripping away years of learned behavior, so be fearless and brave.

Once you've finished column 3, move on to column 4. Column 4 is an opportunity to use free-writing to uncover your past experiences. This is a very powerful and possibly uncomfortable step. Take it slow and trust that you're being guided. Begin by listing all the possible triggers, past wounds, or traumatic events that may be the cause of the judgment noted in column 1. Some of these might be crystal clear. For instance, maybe you judge your boss for the way he treats you, which makes you feel weak and powerless.

Then by the time you hit column 4 it becomes clear to you that this judgment and pain represent an old memory of being reprimanded by your dad. Your anger toward your dad has caused you to have major authority issues. These fears around authority figures have led you to judge and attack in order to feel safe.

While some of your judgments, like the example above, might be pretty easy to unpack, there are likely to be others that you'll resist. Let's call out resistance right now. When your ego feels threatened or in any way afraid of unraveling an old grievance or traumatic wound, you will shut down. You'll go numb and you may even fall asleep. When I began to heal my own judgment, some traumatic memories surfaced for me. Each time I'd try to recall any memories or reasons for my grievance, I'd literally start yawning and fall asleep! This was my brain's way of protecting me from moving too quickly into the uncomfortable feelings and memories. I tell you this because if you find yourself shutting down or feeling exhausted, frustrated, annoyed, or dismissive, it's okay to return to column 4 at a later time. If you can get through only columns 1 through 3 for now, that's fine. You will revisit column 4 when you feel safer. And if this work triggers you in any way, you can also seek professional counseling or access one of the trauma resources I offer at GabbyBernstein.com/bookresources.

Give yourself the time you need to complete all four columns. Once you complete them, take some time to reflect
on what you've uncovered. Answer the following questions
in your journal:

Are there any patterns in your judgment?

Did anything you uncovered surprise you?

How does it make you feel to witness your judgment?

Did you judge yourself for your own judgment?

Did it bring you relief to look at the judgment?

Did it make you uncomfortable to look at the judgment?

Let your pen flow as you answer each question in your
journal. Don't edit anything. Once you've completed each
answer, write down anything else that came up for you. Take
a close look at what this exercise ignited in you and honor
your work.

Throughout this detox, continue to fill in the four columns. Make it part of your daily practice. Each morning
when you wake up, check in and see if you have any new
judgments that you want to witness. I find that if I watch the
news or even scroll through Twitter before bed, I'm likely to
wake up really judgmental. This practice helps me cleanse
that judgment before I begin my day.

Practicing this step first thing in the morning can have a

major impact on your day. Upon waking, take a few minutes to fill in the four-step chart. When you put pen to paper and witness your judgment, it's like throwing open the curtains to your mind and letting the sun pour in. Instead of unconsciously carrying the judgment with you throughout the day, you're shining light on it. The simple act of looking at your judgment can help you begin to feel less attached to it and can set you up to win for the rest of the day.

Throughout the day you're going to continue to judge, as we all do. But now you'll be aware of it, and you'll be amazed by how judgmental you really are. So pay attention to your judgmental thoughts, words, and actions throughout the day. Maybe jot them down in your journal so that you can revisit them later. Try your best to stay committed to the practice of conscious awareness. Remember: The more you look at your judgment, the less attached to it you will be. Witnessing your judgment takes away its power.

Before bed, revisit the four columns and add any new judgments that came up during the day. Each morning and night take time to pay close attention to the judgments that come through. You may find that you have one or two judgments on repeat. You might discover that when one judgment gets resolved, you pick up another to obsess over. Or maybe the same judgment you woke up with is still lingering before you go to sleep. Simply witness your judgment without judgment and take notes in your journal. Continue to pay attention to the patterns and stories that surface.

Throughout this step, keep your focus on your own healing and off other people's behavior. As you look more closely at your judgments you'll be tempted to fixate on all the ways other people are disappointing you and the reasons they should change. Do your best to let them off the hook. Put the grievance on the shelf and place your focus instead on your own healing. Your ego will continually tempt you to project your discomfort onto others. Just lovingly witness the ego's tricks and do your best not to act on them. And when you do (because you will), simply add the new judgment to your list and continue with the practice. Don't worry about how to handle other people. We'll get to that in later steps. For now, focus on your own judgmental habits and let everyone else do their thing.

CELEBRATE THE MIRACLE MOMENTS

This first step in the Judgment Detox will help you become aware of the ways in which judgment wreaks havoc in your subconscious mind. You must become intimately aware of your judgmental patterns in order to heal them. The more mindful you are of how you judge, the easier the following steps will be. Honor yourself for being willing to look at this behavior. Create a section in your journal to celebrate the miracle moments. A miracle moment can be as simple as having the willingness to witness your judgment throughout the day. It can be the recognition that you no longer believe in a judgmental thought. Maybe the miracle is that the judgmental thought troubling you in the morning was gone when you reviewed your notes in the evening. Document your progress throughout the book—and begin now by acknowledging your willingness to look at your judgment, even when it's uncomfortable.

The more consciously aware you become of how judgment shows up in your life, the more willing you will be to continue on this path. You can't heal your perceptions if you're unwilling to look at them.

Five days after the 2016 election I gave a talk at a spiritual expo. The title of my talk was "The Universe Has Your Back," based on lessons from my last book. I got on the stage and opened with a very bold remark. I said, "Given the state we are in, I feel called to change the direction of my talk. I can't stand here today and ignore the division, separation, and judgment that is plaguing our country. I have to speak up. This is not a talk on politics. This is a talk on oneness. This is a time for us to witness our judgment without judgment."

While I didn't give a political talk, the timing was such that politics was on everyone's mind. Among the hundreds of people in the room, there were many strongly held and divergent political viewpoints. Nevertheless, I spent two hours teaching lessons on how we dissolve all boundaries with love, release separation, and show up with more light. I knew that changing the topic of my talk might upset some people, but in the midst of the palpable turmoil, I felt the need to offer guidance, wisdom, and solutions. I did my best to honor both sides of the conversation and bring the conversation back to love and healing.

During the question-and-answer period, a young woman got up and shared about her devastation over the election results. She said, "What upsets me most is how much hate and anger I'm seeing online. People are judging one another for their views. I just want to bring more love to the conversation. What do I do?" I replied, "Post that. Call out the judgment. Shine a light on it by pointing it out. Witness your judgment publicly and share that you want to bring more love to the conversation." She felt empowered by the idea that she didn't have to "do" anything other than acknowledge her own judgment and get honest. She accepted that by telling the truth, she could be set free.

The talk came to an end, and I asked the audience if anyone in the room had a burning desire. Another young woman raised her hand. She said, "Gabby, at the beginning of this talk I almost walked out. I was terrified that you were going to push your political views onto us. I voted for Trump. I am a woman, I've survived three rapes, and I've had a lot of odds stacked against me. But with all that, I've chosen to get behind a man who I believe will bring the change I want. I am standing here proud to say that." The room was silent. I looked at the audience and said, "Let's honor her for her choice and commend her for her bravery to speak up." Then an audience of strangers, the majority of whom likely disagreed with her political views, got up and honored her for her decision with a standing ovation. In that moment the group dissolved their boundaries with love. Having spent two hours in prayer, meditation, and communication with God, they'd looked closely at their fear and judgment, and they chose again. They chose to take judgment off the altar and replace it with love.

I accepted that the direction of my talk may have triggered some people, and I took full responsibility for that. But I was called to speak up about the division and separation we were suffering. This is a time for oneness, and it is my mission to spread that message in whatever way I can.

That's what I believe you're here for. You opened this book because your higher self is guiding you to show up in a greater way—to be more kind, more compassionate, and more loving. The clearest way to find joy and success is to join your mind with love. Love can dissolve all boundaries, separation, war, and attack. When one person chooses love, it's felt throughout the world. Your commitment to this practice matters. It's time to witness your judgment and choose again.

Witnessing your judgment is an act of self-love and a major step toward healing. Your willingness to lovingly look at your judgment has prepared you for the next step, which is to honor your wounds. When you become brave enough to look at your fragmented psyche, it becomes easier to honor the wounds. In the coming lesson you will be guided to look more closely at the wounds that live beneath your judgmental nature. Trust that your willingness to witness your judgment without judgment has prepared you. As you move into this next step, continue to call on Step 1 for help. Remain the nonjudgmental witness of your judgment and trust in the next right action.

Honor the Wound

It can be scary and disorienting to let go of judgment, because it's a pattern we've grown to rely on. In some ways, releasing judgment can feel like letting go of a friend who deep down you know is not good for you. Even though your heart tells you it's time to move on, you feel a sense of sadness and loss.

Underneath every judgment is a core wound. Even the most minor and seemingly insignificant judgments stem from our own shame and shadows. Remember: If we were happy and complete, we wouldn't judge. Our feelings of unworthiness lead us to project judgment outward. Unconsciously we believe that if we put our pain onto someone else, we won't have to feel it. So instead of addressing our own feelings of inadequacy and unworthiness, we avoid our pain by fixating on what we perceive to be the shortcomings of others. But projecting our judgment onto other people gives us only a temporary and tenuous reprieve. Not only do our own feelings of inadequacy *not* dissolve, but to make matters worse, we feel an unconscious (or conscious) guilt for judging others too.

In Step 1 you began to look at the wounds that live beneath the surface of your judgment. You took an honest audit of the feelings, memories, traumas, and experiences that make you feel separate, less than, and afraid. You fearlessly witnessed your judgment without judgment.

With this new awareness of your judgment you're ready to take a bold step in the healing process by honoring your wounds. This has been the most important step in my own recovery process. My willingness to honor my wounds is what has helped me create significant, sustainable change in my judgmental patterns and in my life. I'll be honest: I resisted this practice at first. I wanted to push past the wounds and just get rid of the judgment altogether. But avoidance simply doesn't work. If we don't honor the wounds and energetic patterns that dwell beneath our judgment, they will keep coming up—over and over and over again.

For years I witnessed my judgment with disdain. I felt like a fraud. Here I was, a spiritual teacher who judged *all the time.* I was ashamed of this behavior and continually prayed for miraculous relief from my judgment. I desperately wanted to let go of the habit of judgment, but my good intentions were not enough. Time after time judgment would get the best of me. I'd witness myself speaking negatively about someone for no reason or getting outraged and judgmental about something I saw on the news. These low-vibe thoughts really dragged me down.

I felt helpless and exhausted by my addiction to judgment. But there was a glimmer of hope: Deep down I knew there was a spiritual solution to this problem. My willingness to witness the judgment and my desire to release it were enough to guide me to the next step. I took an honest inventory of the feelings, limiting beliefs, and experiences that lived beneath the surface of my judgment. This practice helped me see the patterns. For instance, while practicing Step 1, I could see clearly how my judgment of know-it-alls stemmed from the time my sixth-grade crush told me I was stupid.

While some of the patterns of judgment were easy to identify, others were harder to spot. I struggled to understand one in particular, or even to admit that this was a judgment of mine at all. I noticed that I was judging women for being flirtatious and sexy. I was embarrassed to even witness this judgment because it brought up a lot of uncomfortable feelings; I was unwilling to explore what lurked behind the pattern.

Then the Universe did for me what I could not do for myself, and I was guided to face the uncomfortable pattern once and for all. Here is how it happened. I was hired to teach at a four-day retreat, but for the first time I wasn't just hosting and teaching—I was also participating. This was a new dynamic for me; up till then I'd always been in "teacher mode." At this event I knew many of the forty-five attendees, and there was a real camaraderie among the group. There was ample free time for everyone to get to know one another and hang out. Within the group was one young woman who was really triggering me. She was beautiful, young, smart, fun, and confident. She was extremely comfortable in her body and exuded a powerful energy that was childlike and sexy at the same time. I wanted to love her, but I couldn't stop judging her in my mind. I kept thinking, *She's such a flirt!*

My judgments got harsher and harsher. It was only a matter of time before I verbalized the negative thoughts. See, the thing is, I'm a big talker. If I think something over and over, it will eventually spill out of my mouth in an inappropriate way.

And it did.

One evening at dinner I walked past the young woman talking to a guy at a table. They were surrounded by a big group of people. I looked at her and said very loudly, "Wow, you're such a flirt!" In that moment I saw utter shock and embarrassment fall over her face. Her energy shut down and she turned her back to me.

I thought, *Oh, God, I really screwed up.* I instantly went into a state of shame and guilt. I could see how she reverberated to my judgment and how much I'd upset her. I felt embarrassed. I was especially ashamed that as one of the presenters at the retreat I would treat someone that way. My judgment had gotten the best of me.

Internally I knew I'd done something wrong, but it took me a while to admit it. At first I wanted to play it down and pretend that it wasn't a big deal. I didn't want to own up to the fact I'd done something so crappy. But deep down I knew that I had projected a deep wound of my own onto this innocent woman. I woke up the next day still feeling extreme shame and guilt. I texted her and said, "Let's meet for breakfast." She replied, "Good idea."

We sat down for breakfast and I broke the ice by saying, "I'm sorry if I offended you last night—I was just kidding around." But my non-apology apology was understandably not enough for her. She told me how upset she was by the way I treated her and that she felt it wasn't a joke. She felt that it was backed up with some kind of nasty resentment.

Her response resonated. And it made me feel even more ashamed. In that shame I had two choices. I could continue to defend myself and give her a half-assed apology, or I could take a good look at the true reasons behind my judgment. I wasn't sure which direction I was going to go in, so instead I prayed. I silently asked spirit to step in and intervene.

In my silence she spoke again. She said, "You know, what you said upset me deeply because I have a lot of shame around getting male attention." She went on to share that she had recently uncovered troubling memories from her childhood that made her feel ashamed of male attention.

This was the miracle moment. I sat across from this innocent woman and shared with her that only three months earlier I too had remembered my own childhood trauma. I admitted that for more than thirty years I'd been living with guilt and shame around my sexuality. And in that moment I witnessed my wound. I apologized sincerely and fully, and I said, "Your sexual freedom triggered my shame. It made me feel like I wasn't good enough and that something was wrong with me. That's why I judged you." In that moment our truth was exposed and we honored our wounds. We stood up in the busy breakfast hall surrounded by people and we held each other and cried. We cried for our childhood trauma, we cried for our lost innocence, and we cried with joy for the healing we were receiving.

This moment of truth dissolved the separation and attack. Being brave enough to honor our wounds made the judgment fade away. We recognized our own wounds, shame, and triggers in each other. By honoring those wounds, we were set free.

I know this moment was divinely guided. I trust that God was leading me to this spiritual assignment to show me an unhealed part of my shadow. Remember that even though we're always being guided, we can always exercise free will. In that moment I could have shrunk in the darkness of my shadow or risen up to the light. I chose to rise.

This spiritual assignment helped me honor my wound, but there was more work to do. Examining my feelings closely, I could begin to see that my reaction to being scared, feeling inadequate, and needing protection wasn't actually present-day me. Instead, there was an innocent child desperately trying to protect herself from feeling shame and fear.

My newfound awareness of the pain behind my judgment helped me see myself with a lot of love and compassion. I honored myself for being brave enough to look at this darkness and identify it as the cause of my behavior. I could see clearly how my attempts to avoid my unhealed shame and suffering led me to project it outward. I projected it onto my friends, my husband, and even strangers. I spent my life judging the world around me to avoid feeling the shame inside. This revelation was huge for me. It made me realize how much sadness I was running from and how judgment was my greatest defense for avoiding the truth.

In order to be free from this old pattern I had to honor my wounds. As the Universe would have it, right when I was ready to heal more, I was presented with the perfect opportunity for recovery. At the time I was deeply committed to working through my memories of childhood trauma. I had built a team of therapists, energy healers, and personal growth practitioners to help me. One of the healing modalities that brought me great relief was EFT, Emotional Freedom Techniques. This is also known as tapping, and I'll use these terms interchangeably.

EFT is a psychological acupressure technique that supports your emotional health. EFT is unique in bringing together the cognitive benefits of therapy with the physical benefits of acupuncture to restore your energy and heal your emotions. EFT does not use needles. You simply stimulate certain meridian points on the body by tapping on them with your fingertips.

More than five thousand years ago, the Chinese recognized a series of energy circuits that run through the body. They called these circuits *meridians,* and today this concept is the basis for acupuncture and acupressure healing. When you tap on specific energy meridians found on your face, head, arm, and chest, you can release old fears, limiting beliefs, negative patterns, and even physical pain. While you tap, you talk out loud about the issue you are working to heal. Allowing yourself to emote while simultaneously tapping on the energy points sends a signal to the brain that it's safe to relax. Our fear response, which is controlled by the amygdala, is lessened.

The goal of EFT is to balance disturbances in your energy field, not unearth any specific memory. Great healing and relief can come without having to relive any memories at all.

Gary Craig, who created EFT, has said, "The cause of all negative emotions is a disruption in the body's energy system." Gary teaches that the negative emotion is not caused by a traumatic memory or experience; it's caused by a traumatic event that *creates a disruption in the body's energy system.* In turn, that disruption creates negative emotion. Through the process of EFT, you can heal the disruption in your energy system, thereby healing the emotions.

As Gary puts it:

EFT operates on the premise that no matter what part of your life needs improvement, there are unresolved emotional issues in the way. . . . The EFT premise also includes the understanding that the more unresolved emotional issues you can clear, the more peace and emotional freedom you will have in your life. . . . With that in mind, EFT can be an ongoing process that we use to clear out the old traumas, and welcome any new challenges with a healthy, productive attitude.

This technique will help you uncover the root cause of your judgment and mend the energy disruption that made you feel the need to judge in the first place. Negative experiences caused the energy disruption, and your response to that disruption was fear—which you avoided feeling by projecting it outward through judgment. To heal the projection, you must heal the disruption.

There is relatively little emotional suffering involved in the practice of EFT, especially compared with some traditional therapy methods. In part, that's why I love teaching this technique. I have found that tapping is one of the most powerful ways to bust through the blocks, relieve physical pain, release phobias, and heal the negative emotions behind traumatic experiences. It's also easy to learn and can be practiced anywhere, anytime. Through the process of tapping you can experience miraculous shifts—and the shifts can happen fast.

The EFT practice is simple. Follow my guidance below and stay open to receive healing.

Ready to start healing? Here's how it works.

Whenever you begin the tapping process you start with what's called the Most Pressing Issue, or MPI. In this case the MPI is related to judgment. Let's start with the phrase "I can't stop judging this person." You can modify this to make it specific to your own situation. The "person" may be one individual, a group of people, or even you yourself. You can modify the script below to best suit your situation.

Next, you rate your pre-tapping MPI on a scale of 0 to 10, 10 being the most distressing. We rate the MPI before we start tapping because of what is known as the Apex Effect phenomenon, in which people tend to discount or dismiss the actual benefit of tapping. After completing a tapping session, people frequently experience many of the desired outcomes, including the release of fear, pain, or other symptoms associated with their MPI. However, sometimes people who are new to tapping don't credit these benefits to the Emotional Freedom Techniques. Instead, they tend to come up with excuses as to why their symptoms are gone. They might think they were sufficiently distracted, or that something happened during the process that made them smile or laugh, which "did the trick." Some people can even forget that they had the symptoms at all! One minute they can be terrified by a phobia of heights and the next minute insist that heights are not a problem. It sounds a little weird, but EFT practitioners see it happen all the time. And the risk of failing to recognize the benefit of EFT is that it may keep you from turning to this powerful healing technique when it could help you greatly.

To avoid the Apex Effect, we rate the MPI from 0 to 10 before we tap. This 0 to 10 number gives you a definitive reference point you can refer back to after your session. (And in case you're curious, yes: People can begin a session at a 10 and tap down to a 0 within minutes.) Rating your MPI will help you avoid the Apex Effect and will give you a chance to celebrate your healing and success.

While the tapping process can sound a little strange at first, it's actually really simple. I've used this technique to rid myself of physical pain and to deal with minor grievances and even serious traumas and phobias. For a while I suffered from a terrible fear of elevators. I'd gotten stuck in two elevators in the span of six months. Those experiences triggered earlier life fears and ultimately made it so I couldn't set foot in an elevator. I would walk up twenty flights of stairs before I'd even consider getting into an elevator. This fear was becoming unmanageable, so I had to do something about it. I decided to tap on it. In just a few tapping sessions I was able to get to the root cause of my trauma and heal the disruption of energy. The following day I got into an elevator with absolutely no concern at all. It was a miracle.

Throughout this step in the Judgment Detox I will guide you to use tapping to help you heal the energetic disturbances, feelings, resentments, and traumas that dwell beneath your judgmental patterns. Remember, the reason you judge is because you're avoiding an emotion that you don't want to feel. Once you begin to tap on the underlying wound, you will release the energetic disruption in your body and will feel emotionally free. In that space of emotional freedom, you'll no longer need to judge others or yourself. Tapping will help you clear space for the deeper spiritual healing that is presented in the coming chapters. You must heal the energetic disruption that lives below the pattern in order to shift your behavior.

When you begin your tapping practice, it helps to follow a script. The following scripts will guide you to explore the emotions behind your judgment. Say each line out loud while you tap on the corresponding meridian point. You can tap with either hand, and it doesn't matter which side of your face or body you tap on. The script will guide you through a few rounds in which you'll honor your fear, resentment, and discomfort. These are called negative rounds. Then, as you start to feel a little relief from the negative rounds, you'll move into positive rounds by shifting the patterns around those thoughts. The shift from negative to positive will feel great. Your body will relax, your breath will deepen, and you'll likely loosen your grip on any justification for your judgment. You may even let go of it entirely.

To help you begin your EFT journey, I've written a specific tapping script that works directly on the issue of judgment. Use the script below and tap on the designated areas of your body (meridian points) as you say the suggested phrases. Before you begin, review each meridian point in the following image.

TAPPING FOR JUDGMENT

We start by rating your MPI. Ask yourself how emotionally charged you are when you think about the person you can't stop judging. (Remember the person can be a group of people or even yourself. You can replace the words *this person* with a name.)

Rate your MPI from 0 to 10, 10 being the most emotionally charged.

Tapping Points

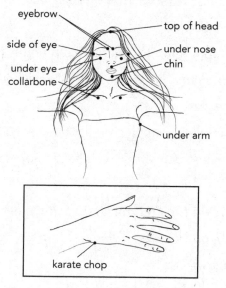

eyebrow
top of head
side of eye
under nose
under eye
chin
collarbone

under arm

karate chop

Your MPI rating: _____

The next step is to begin tapping on the karate chop point (as seen in the illustration above) with your other hand. While tapping, repeat the following phrase out loud three times: *Even though I can't stop judging this person, I deeply and completely love and accept myself.*

While tapping on the karate chop point: *Even though I can't stop judging this person, I deeply and completely love and accept myself.*

While tapping on the karate chop point: *Even though I can't stop judging this person, I deeply and completely love and accept myself.*

While tapping on the karate chop point: *Even though I can't stop judging this person, I deeply and completely love and accept myself.*

Continue lightly tapping on the other meridians one by one while saying each phrase out loud. Follow this sequence:

Tapping on the eyebrow: I can't stop judging.

Tapping on the side of the eye: It feels so good to judge them.

Tapping under the eye: Judging makes me feel better about myself.

Tapping under the nose: And this person really deserves my judgment.

Tapping on the chin: They've done so much to make me want to judge.

Tapping on the collarbone: They deserve it, after all.

Tapping under the arm: I feel justified in my judgment.

Tapping on top of the head: They deserve it!

Tapping on the eyebrow: If I give up judgment, I will be giving in.

Tapping on the side of the eye: I don't want to stop judging.

Tapping under the eye: Judging makes me feel better about myself.

Tapping under the nose: I believe I deserve to judge them for this.

Tapping on the chin: They've made me really upset.

Tapping on the collarbone: They've really gotten under my skin.

Tapping under the arm: They deserve it!

Tapping on top of the head: They deserve it!

Tapping on the eyebrow: They've upset me so much!

Tapping on the side of the eye: I deserve to judge them for what they've done.

Tapping under the eye: I just can't let it go.

Tapping under the nose: How could someone be that way?

Tapping on the chin: I'm so triggered by them.

Tapping on the collarbone: I'm so annoyed.

Tapping under the arm: I'm so aggravated by them.

Tapping on top of the head: They deserve it!

Tapping on the eyebrow: All this judgment.

Tapping on the side of the eye: I feel it's justified after all they've done.

Tapping under the eye: I have so many reasons to judge this person.

Tapping under the nose: It feels good to judge them.

Tapping on the chin: I feel safe when I judge them.

Tapping on the collarbone: I judge to protect myself.

Tapping under the arm: I need to do that because deep down I feel shame.

Tapping on top of the head: I want to heal my shame.

Tapping on the eyebrow: All this shame.

Tapping on the side of the eye: I don't even want to acknowledge it.

Tapping under the eye: I have to judge to avoid this shame.

Tapping under the nose: It feels safer to judge.

Tapping on the chin: I'm afraid of my shame, so I judge.

Tapping on the collarbone: I'm afraid of my shame.

Tapping under the arm: But I want to release it.

Tapping on top of the head: I want to heal my shame so I can stop judging.

Continue to tap through the negative rounds outlined above. The moment you feel a sense of relief, you can begin the positive rounds:

Tapping on the eyebrow: But judgment doesn't really make me feel better.

Tapping on the side of the eye: Love actually makes me feel a lot better.

Tapping under the eye: But judging just seems easier.

Tapping under the nose: If I released judgment, who would I be?

Tapping on the chin: I guess I'd be left with me.

Tapping on the collarbone: Being me may be better.

Tapping under the arm: I have to release judgment to love myself again.

Tapping on the top of the head: If I release them, I will be free.

Tapping on the eyebrow: All the energy I spend judging could be spent on feeling good.

Tapping on the side of the eye: I could use the energy more wisely.

Tapping under the eye: And I could increase my energy by choosing to love rather than judge.

Tapping under the nose: I can also see that I'm judging a person who is in pain.

Tapping under the chin: I can see them with compassion.

Tapping on the collarbone: I can see that they're in pain.

Tapping under the arm: I want to send them love and prayers.

Tapping on top of the head: They just want to be happy. Just like me.

Tapping on the eyebrow: I want to be happy.

Tapping on the side of the eye: Releasing judgment sets me free to be happy.

Tapping under the eye: I'd much rather feel free.

Tapping under the nose: I choose to send love to this person.

Tapping on the chin: That love will clear my blocks.

Tapping on the collarbone: And I will feel that freedom.

Tapping under the arm: I choose love.

Tapping on top of the head: I choose to be free from judgment.

Tapping on the eyebrow: I want to be happy and free.

Tapping on the side of the eye: I want to forgive so I can feel good.

Tapping under the eye: I don't want to feel judgmental anymore.

Tapping under the nose: I pray for this person to feel good too.

Tapping on the chin: That love will clear my blocks.

Tapping on the collarbone: All I want is happiness.

Tapping under the arm: I choose happiness.
Tapping on the top of the head: I choose to be free
   from judgment.

Tap through the positive statements as many times as you'd like until you feel genuine relief.

When you're done, say your MPI out loud: "I can't stop judging this person." Now rate it from 0 to 10 and compare it to when you first began. If you tapped through each round with commitment, you're sure to have experienced relief. In some cases you may drop from a 10 to a 2 in just a minute of tapping, though any relief is a miracle! This tool is one of the most powerful ways to bust through blocks in an instant.

If you didn't feel relief, then keep tapping. Keep tapping, and in time you'll feel immense relief.

Once you're finished with your positive rounds and have stated your MPI out loud, rate it again here: _____

Remember, if you didn't feel relief right away, you can continue tapping or return to the process when you're ready.

It's possible your Most Pressing Issue isn't around judging others. Maybe your MPI is that you feel judged (which may also make you judge others). So consequently you may feel justified in your thoughts. But remember that judgment is a cycle, so defending yourself with judgment is really no different than initiating the judgment. The tapping script below will help you heal your feelings of being judged. When you heal the feeling of being judged, you'll no longer feel the need to protect yourself by judging others. You can free yourself from it now. Let's tap on that feeling.

TAPPING FOR FEELING JUDGED

Begin by stating your MPI: "I feel judged."

Your MPI rating:_____

Now let's begin by saying the initial statement three times out loud while you tap the karate chop point: *Even though I feel judged, I deeply and completely love and accept myself.*

Karate chop point: *Even though I feel judged, I deeply and completely love and accept myself.*

Karate chop point: *Even though I feel judged, I deeply and completely love and accept myself.*

Karate chop point: *Even though I feel judged, I deeply and completely love and accept myself.*

Continue with a few negative rounds:

Eyebrow: I feel so judged.

Side of eye: This judgment makes me so mad.

Under eye: How dare they judge me.

Under nose: They're the one who're really wrong.
Not me.

Chin: They think they're better than me.

Collarbone: What's wrong with them?

Under arm: Why do they think they're better than me?

Top of head: Who do they think they are?

Eyebrow: How dare they judge me like that?

Side of eye: They're the one with the problem.

Under eye: I'm innocent in this.

Under nose: I don't deserve to be judged.

Chin: How dare they judge me?!

Collarbone: What's wrong with them?

Under arm: They're not better than me.

Top of head: But their judgment makes me feel small.

Eyebrow: Their judgment makes me feel less than.

Side of eye: I feel like I'm not good enough.

Under eye: I feel terrible about myself.

Under nose: And because I feel so bad about myself, I
want to judge them back.

Chin: It makes me feel better to judge them back.

Collarbone: I feel justified in my judgment.

Under arm: They deserve it.

Top of head: Because they judged me first.

Eyebrow: I'm so angry with them.

Side of eye: They make me feel terrible.

Under eye: They make me feel shame.

Under nose: They make me feel wrong and I know I'm
    not wrong.

Chin: I judge them to protect myself.

Collarbone: I feel justified in my judgment.

Under arm: They deserve it.

Top of head: Because they judged me first.

Continue tapping on the negative rounds until you feel
some relief. At that point you can move into the positive
rounds and begin tapping.

Eyebrow: I no longer want to feel judged.

Side of eye: It really sucks.

Under eye: I want to feel better.

Under nose: The more I focus on their judgment, the
    worse I feel.

Chin: The more I obsess about their judgment, the
    more I want to judge.

Collarbone: I don't want to judge.

Under arm: If I stop judging them, then I can feel better.

Top of head: The only reason they judge me is because they feel shame.

Eyebrow: Happy people don't judge others.

Side of eye: If they're not happy, I actually feel bad for them.

Under eye: I know they just want to feel good.

Under nose: They're just like me.

Chin: They want to feel good.

Collarbone: All we want is to feel good.

Under arm: I want to pray for them to feel good too.

Top of head: They're sad, and all they want is to feel good.

Eyebrow: They are just like me.

Side of eye: They just want to be happy.

Under eye: We are the same.

Under nose: I can see them as me.

Chin: They're just protecting themselves too.

Collarbone: They just want to feel better.

Under arm: I want to feel better.

Top of head: We all deserve to feel better now.

Eyebrow: They just want to feel good.

Side of eye: Just like me.

Under eye: We are the same.

Under nose: *I can forgive them for judging because they just feel terrible.*

Chin: *Why else would they judge?*

Collarbone: *I want them to feel better.*

Under arm: *I want to feel better.*

Top of head: *I deserve to feel better now.*

Take a deep breath and release. Now restate your MPI: "I feel judged." And from a scale of 0 to 10, where are you?

Your MPI rating: _____

TAPPING FOR SHAME

The wounds that live beneath our judgment are often backed with paralyzing feelings of shame. Shame is a very difficult emotion. It's one that we might never even acknowledge because we're too afraid to even admit it's there. When these wounds are triggered, we go straight to judgment to avoid the feeling of shame. The ego convinces us that if we were to address our shame we'd fall apart. It tells us there's just no way we could confront our shame without wrecking our sense of self. So instead we bury our shame in the judgmental stories that we project outward.

It took me years to even acknowledge my shame, and

my fear of facing it kept me stuck in the judgment cycle. Through the process of tapping on my wounds I was able to uncover that the feeling lurking beneath my wounds was shame. It was the tapping process that brought my shame to the light. For decades I ran from shame. I avoided it at all costs. But through EFT I was able to bring it to the surface for healing in a way that felt safe. Tapping on my shame led me to life-changing relief.

It's possible that tapping on your judgment helped you witness your shame. Or maybe it created more resistance. Shame has been running the show for far too long. It's time to tap on your shame so that you can truly understand, honor, and heal the root of your judgment.

Let's tap on the MPI "I feel shame." State the MPI out loud.

Now rate your MPI from 0 to 10.

Your MPI rating:_____

Let's begin with the setup statement. While tapping on the karate chop point, repeat the following phrase out loud three times: *Even though I feel shame, I deeply and completely love and accept myself.*

Karate chop point: *Even though I feel shame, I deeply and completely love and accept myself.*

Karate chop point: *Even though I feel shame, I deeply and completely love and accept myself.*

Karate chop point: *Even though I feel shame, I deeply and completely love and accept myself.*

Continue lightly tapping on the other meridians one by one while saying each point out loud. Follow this sequence:

Eyebrow: *I feel shame.*

Side of eye: *And I'm terrified of it.*

Under eye: *I really do not want to feel this shame.*

Under nose: *I'll do anything to avoid this feeling.*

Chin: *I hate this process.*

Collarbone: *I do not want to acknowledge this shame.*

Under arm: *I'm ashamed to even look at this.*

Top of head: *I'd rather judge than feel shame.*

Eyebrow: *It's so uncomfortable.*

Side of eye: *All this shame.*

Under eye: *I just want to run from it.*

Under nose: *I want to avoid it.*

Chin: *It's terrifying to admit my shame.*

Collarbone: *Shame feels heavy.*

Under arm: *Shame makes me sad.*

Top of head: *I'd rather judge than feel shame.*

Eyebrow: *I want to keep running from my shame.*

Side of eye: But I know I can't.

Under eye: It always shows up again.

Under nose: I can't avoid it.

Chin: Shame has been running the show.

Collarbone: Shame has made me run.

Under arm: I'm ready to stop running.

Top of head: I'm ready to face my shame.

Continue tapping on the negative rounds until you feel some relief. At that point you can move into the positive rounds and begin tapping.

Eyebrow: Even though I feel this shame, I love myself.

Side of eye: I honor the shame.

Under eye: I've been through so much and it's been scary.

Under nose: I understand how I could feel shame.

Chin: I feel compassion for myself.

Collarbone: I honor my shame.

Under arm: And I'm ready to stop running from it.

Top of head: It actually feels good to bring my shame to the surface.

Eyebrow: Feeling my shame brings me relief.

Side of eye: I no longer feel like I need to run from it.

Under eye: I feel relief.

Under nose: I want this relief more than anything.

Chin: I can change my relationship to shame.

Collarbone: When I honor my shame, I no longer need
 to run from it.

Under arm: Wow! I no longer need to run.

Top of head: That feels awesome.

Eyebrow: It's safe to feel my shame.

Side of eye: I can have a new relationship to my
 shame.

Under eye: I can feel it and heal it.

Under nose: I can stop running.

Chin: I can stop judging.

Collarbone: I can honor my shame.

Under arm: I can feel shame and love myself anyway.

Top of head: I can truly love myself no matter what.

Take a deep breath and release. Now restate your MPI:
"I feel shame." And from a scale of 0 to 10, where are you?

Your MPI rating: _____

I imagine that you're feeling great relief. The wonderful
thing about tapping is that the more you do it, the better you
feel. If you've tapped down an issue from 10 to 0, you don't

need to tap on it again. New aspects of the issue may present themselves to you, at which point you can tap on them. But it is possible to completely tap an issue down to 0 and never have to revisit it again.

Remember that this is a process of healing the disruption of energy. You don't have to dig up all the difficult memories from your past. You just need the willingness to talk about the judgment and tap on the meridians. Follow these steps and trust in the process.

To enhance your experience of EFT I suggest that you practice tapping at least once a day for thirty days. You can reference your list of judgments from Step 1 and tap on a new judgment each day for thirty days. If new judgments come up, just add them to the list. It doesn't matter how big or small the issue is, just tap on it. Don't worry about what you're "meant" to tap on. The moment you witness a judgment, practice Step 1 to become more aware of the pattern of unconscious feelings underneath the judgment. Then practice Step 2: Tap on it. Day by day, tap down each judgment. You may feel the need to tap on the same judgment for a few days in a row, but hopefully once you tap on an issue, it can be resolved. Start by using the scripts in this chapter, and in time you'll begin to guide yourself with your own words. Always follow the sequence of meridian points shown above when tapping—the order in which you tap each point always remains the same. Remember also to take yourself through a few negative rounds, and then when you're ready, move into the positive rounds. The more you practice EFT, the more intuitive it will become. Don't worry if you feel a little awkward at first. Trust in the process and expect miracles.

Over the next thirty days you'll likely move onto the next steps in this detox. Keep tapping and add in the additional steps as they are presented. The Judgment Detox process has a cumulative effect. One step at a time you get closer and closer to freedom.

You may find that EFT is bringing you a lot of relief and you want to apply it to other issues beyond judgment. By all means, do it! Tapping is fantastic for healing emotional trauma, physical pain, and resentments. In this book we are tapping on judgment, but if you're redirected to other emotional issues, EFT still has a positive effect on reducing judgment. Physical pain, emotional trauma, and many other issues that arise tend to trigger our desire to judge and thus to avoid pain. Therefore, healing whatever pain is present through the tapping process will seriously benefit you as you go through the Judgment Detox. Regardless of the underlying issue, the freedom that comes from tapping will support your Judgment Detox.

Reflect for a moment on the brave step you've taken.

Your willingness to witness your judgment and honor the wounds is the hardest part of this practice. By recognizing and healing the disruption of energy underneath the wound, we forge a pathway to healing the root cause of our judgment.

I hope that throughout this healing journey you start to learn to trust your intuition. If you intuitively feel that you need to tap on something, then tap on it! Trust that whatever comes up for you is divinely guided. Your higher self is working through you to support your healing path. An infinite and loving voice of wisdom resides within each of us—the voice of our inner guide. Your inner guidance system is what led you to pick up this book and read to this point. Begin to trust in the presence of this inner wisdom and don't hesitate to follow its direction. The more you surrender to the good, orderly direction of your inner guide, the more support you'll feel on your healing path. I've grown to rely on this inner voice.

If you're not familiar with the direction of your inner guidance, simply follow the steps in this book and pay attention to the intuitive ideas that come forth. Your intuition may tell you that it's time to tap on a new topic or that you need to add a new judgment to the list. Your intuition may even guide you to slow down the process if it feels like too much to digest at once. Trust your gut throughout this path and you'll heighten your capacity to improve spiritually and emotionally.

We are all innocent, wounded children who have faced many difficulties in our lives. This is true no matter your social status or your background. No one gets through life without some type of wound. And, in fact, our wounds help make us interesting, creative, and unique. But those same wounds also make us neurotic, defensive, and judgmental. When we become brave enough to face our wounds, true healing begins. The Sufi poet Rumi said, "The wound is the place where the light enters you." Follow the guidance of this step and let the light enter in. Even a little light is enough.

In Step 3, you'll begin to strengthen your relationship to your inner guide. This very spiritual part of the process will teach you how to turn over your thoughts, energy, and intention to the care of your inner guidance system. As you do so, I will help you establish a spiritual relationship of your own. You'll be given guidance and practices to surrender your judgments and turn them over to a presence of love beyond your logical mind. Even if this type of language or practice is new to you, I'm certain that you'll feel a lot of relief. Honestly, it doesn't matter whether you're totally new to spirituality or have had a practice for decades—you are ready for this step. Remain open to the process and miraculous results will occur. Just stay willing.

Great relief is available to you in Step 3. Be open, receptive, and willing to let judgment go. You've done amazing work thus far. Take a moment to celebrate the miracles and witness the distance you've already come. It takes bravery, willingness, and a deep desire to give up judgment. Be proud of yourself! Trust and surrender to each step ahead and know you're being guided. This path is perfectly designed for long-lasting relief and happiness.

Put Love on the Altar

Over the past decade I've gotten into a bad habit. As a business owner managing many moving pieces, I have to make a lot of big decisions and often don't have much time to do so. As a result I've developed a pattern of second-guessing my choices. This nasty habit has far-reaching consequences. Whenever I second-guess my decisions, I go into a spiral of judgment and attack. I judge my partners, I judge my team, I judge the decisions I've made, and of course I judge myself. I judge myself for moving too fast. I judge myself for failing to properly think through an issue or for trusting someone else's opinion over my own. To make matters worse, I don't let the judgment go. I've spent weeks, months, and even years obsessing over an outcome that I couldn't control.

Recently I was presented with a major business decision I ended up second-guessing; this sent me into a super-negative judgmental spiral. It involved a contract that obligated me to a significant time and workload commitment. I said yes to this opportunity pretty hastily, already slammed with existing work. Within a couple of days, however, I began to have second thoughts about the decision and went into a judgment cycle that lasted several months. I obsessed about it in therapy, complained about it to my husband, and incessantly discussed it with friends who couldn't have cared less. I babbled and judged and dissected. All of this was exhausting and frustrating, but it felt impossible to stop. Underneath all the obsessing was a deep-rooted resentment toward myself that I didn't know how to handle. This judgment cycle was getting the best of me.

Even in the midst of this internal drama I could see how I was projecting my own guilt onto others. I worked hard to justify my judgment, but deep down, I knew I had to let it go. I could see that my blame and resentment were really a projection of how I felt toward myself. I knew I needed to practice acceptance, move on, and focus on more positive aspects of my life. I applied Steps 1 and 2, but these acts weren't enough to get me out of this ego headlock. I needed a spiritual intervention.

I knew deep down that the only solution to this problem

would come from spiritual surrender. So I asked my inner guidance system to reorganize the story for me. I began to pray about it. I prayed every day for spiritual signs and direction on how to let go of the drama. I surrendered and trusted that my prayers were being heard. I remained patient as I awaited the miracle.

Once I'd surrendered through prayer, my constant self-judgment and obsession began to subside. I felt relief and noticed that I was slowly letting go of the need to control. But then one night I couldn't sleep. I lay in bed tossing and turning, uncomfortable and fitful, mentally preoccupied with every little issue out of my control. And then, like clockwork, the story came back into my mind: Boom. For nearly an hour I lay in bed meticulously reviewing all the ways things could have gone differently had I taken more time making my decision. I went down the list of all the people I resented for this outcome and even attacked myself for getting stuck back in the issue. My self-judgment had roared back with a vengeance.

I glanced at the clock and realized that I needed to get up in four hours. I said a prayer: "Inner guide, please help me release this judgment and return to peace." I felt an instant presence of relief come over me. And then—and this was weird—my intuition said, "Turn on the TV." I hate watching TV before bed, but I listened to the guidance and grabbed the remote. On TV was the preacher and televangelist Joel Osteen. For years I'd been a fan of Joel's work from afar, but I'd never watched him preach. When I tuned in, he was onstage in front of thousands of people, televised for millions. The first words out of his mouth were "Do you ever obsess over something that's out of your control?" I practically yelled at the TV, "Yes, Joel, I do!" He went on to explain that when we do this, we inevitably judge ourselves for obsessing over the small stuff, which creates a negative cycle.

Joel talked about how we spend a ton of our time putting what we *don't* want on the altar. When judgment is on the altar, we get stuck in the chaos of what we don't want and only create more of it. When we try to control outcomes, Joel explained, and focus our attention on what's not working, we actually weaken our faith. Instead, we must trust in a higher power completely in order to be free. We must put love on the altar.

I sat up in my bed, hanging on to his every word. I knew my prayer had been answered. I had prayed to release the judgment, so my higher power led me to turn on the TV and get the exact message I needed to receive. It was time for me to release my judgment once and for all and put love back on the altar. I made a commitment that night to release this issue and turn it over to the Universe. I trusted that by offering it up and focusing my attention on love and gratitude, I would be led to feel better. I'd also clear some space to make decisions with ease and end the cycle for good.

Being on a spiritual path for most of my life has shown me that giving my life over to the care of a higher power is far more meaningful than trying to control every detail. But even with all my faith, my practices, and my connection to spirit, I often forget. This night, spirit reminded me of what was real the moment I listened to the guidance and turned on the TV.

We all have a higher power working on our behalf to restore our thoughts back to love. In any given moment we can put love back on the altar and let it shine through any situation or grievance. Love can dissolve even the most deep-rooted judgment.

Love is the antidote to judgment.

I have come to believe that all issues must be brought to spirit for healing. Without a spiritual intervention, we will stay stuck in the judgment cycle. So we call on a spiritual relationship as we understand it to replace our fear-based judgmental thoughts with love. We ask to let love in. When we surrender our issues to a power greater than ourselves, divine order unfolds.

It doesn't matter whether you believe in God, spirit, or the energy of the Universe. All that matters is that you're willing to let go and be free. Your desire to be free from judgment is enough to establish a spiritual connection. Throughout this step, I'm going to ask you to suspend any disbelief you may have and surrender your judgment to a power greater than you. If this is new to you, then get psyched! Endless freedom and grace are available to you when you receive spiritual guidance.

The spiritual guidance I received came through the voice of my inner wisdom. That voice told me to turn on the TV, allowing me to catch Joel Osteen delivering the exact message that I needed to hear. When we say a prayer, we allow our consciousness to receive intuitive guidance. This guidance is available to us all—as long as we ask for it and as long as we slow down enough to hear it.

This step may seem complex to your logical mind. It's only natural that part of you wants to hold on and control. Even if you already pray, you may be using prayer as another way to try to control situations rather than surrender to them. (More on this later.)

We are all familiar with the desire to control. Part of why you judge is to maintain your sense of control and safety. Ironically, this works only to keep judgment in charge. In order to free ourselves from the bondage of judgment, we must learn to rely on a voice beyond our own. We all have inner wisdom, a voice of love and healing that implores us to ask for help. The moment we ask for help through prayer is the moment we open the invisible gate to receive guidance. That guidance shows up when we pray because we attune our awareness to it, and once we're consciously open to receive, guidance can come in many forms. It may come through a song, a book, a friend, a strong intuitive knowing, or a religious leader. There are infinite ways to receive direction, and it doesn't matter how you get there. What matters is that you're willing to ask for help.

If you've never prayed before or haven't done it in a long time, here's something to keep in mind: The desire to release judgment is in itself a prayer. So rest assured that you already know how to pray. When you pray to release judgment, you invite in the presence of a divine intermediary, a spiritual guide whose only job is to heal your judgmental thoughts and build a bridge that leads you back to love. Your inner guide is a loving teacher who knows exactly how to communicate with you so his or her message will resonate. This teacher is creative, wise, and very patient. Even if you initially ignore the guidance, more will be presented to you.

There are many names for this inner wisdom: Holy Spirit, God, Universe, spirit, inner guide. Throughout the book I'll use these terms interchangeably. There are countless ways that your inner wisdom can connect your thoughts back to love, and you'll receive your guidance in a unique form relevant to you. You may find that you tend to receive guidance in one particular form, or it might change depending on the situation and what the Universe knows will catch your attention.

The guidance comes fast when you ask for it. After you pray for help, your job is to pay attention to the direction you receive. Once you get that direction, follow it. But continue to exercise free will and good decision-making. You can receive guidance and choose to turn your back on it or ignore it. Maybe in the moment your judgment still feels justified, or maybe the idea of letting it go makes you feel unsafe. That's fine—just keep praying. In time you will feel relief. As long as you stay surrendered through prayer, you'll learn to adopt the loving guidance you're receiving.

Right now you may have no clue how to pay attention to loving guidance. The idea of receiving it might freak you out or you may feel skeptical. Judgment is your resistance to love. The world you see is an outward projection of an internal condition, and changing the projection is an "inside job." This means that if you want to see the outside world differently, you need to change your thoughts through prayer. In Steps 1 and 2 you looked at your fear-based beliefs and you realized that they weren't what you wanted to experience. You witnessed the decision-making part of your mind that chose fear and judgment. When you find yourself judging, recognize that the judgment is not what you think it is—it is just a way to try to avoid feeling pain, acknowledging past trauma, and exposing wounds. When you become willing to question your judgment and give it over to spirit for help, you begin to adjust your internal condition. When you acknowledge that you have a wrong mind that has chosen judgment and a right mind that is seeking the truth, you begin the journey of healing through prayer. Instead of fighting and struggling against judgment, you can offer it up and accept the potential for internal healing. Accept that you need help in making that shift, and ask for that help through prayer.

It's always helpful to remember that everyone has the same judgmental nature and the same desire to be free. When we acknowledge our judgment as a response to our fear, we can choose to see peace instead. We can offer up our judgment to a higher power and take away its potency, because when we pray, we invite love to enter into our mind and reorganize our beliefs.

Let's learn to rely on the voice of your inner guide, whose

spiritual presence will act as an intermediary to lead your judgmental thoughts back to love.

To help you establish a faithful relationship with your inner guide I've outlined clear practices. Use these practices to open up a dialogue of asking and receiving. Follow my suggested path and pay attention to the guidance you receive.

IDENTIFY A SPECIFIC JUDGMENT YOU WANT TO RELEASE

Take a moment to choose a judgment that's present for you. Maybe you couldn't tap it down with EFT or maybe you've been unwilling to do any work on it so far. This is the judgment that you'll want to offer up to your inner guide through prayer. In a live Judgment Detox workshop I led in 2016, a young woman got on the microphone and said, "Gabby, I love these methods and I'm willing to release judgment toward just about everyone. But there's one person I'm not willing to release. That person is the man who raped me when I was in high school." She wept as she opened up about how she was unwilling to forgive him because her judgment made her feel safe.

I deeply empathized with her fear of releasing the judgment. When someone has hurt you or someone close to you in a serious way, it can feel impossible to let go of your judgment. But as I explained to this young woman who bravely shared her story, failing to release her judgment was actually hurting her. As long as she carried the grievance, she was reliving the trauma every day. While I didn't have a logical explanation for how she would let go of this particular judgment, I knew with all my heart that her desire to be free and her willingness to surrender through prayer were enough. Together, they were all she needed to get on a path toward true freedom and relief. The fact that she spoke up at all told me she was already on her way.

Releasing judgment toward someone who's seriously hurt you or someone you love can almost feel like a betrayal as far as our logical mind is concerned. It can be painful to consider letting go of the judgment, which may be what has kept you feeling safe. But this sense of safety is an illusion. You have to constantly judge the person who hurt you, constantly direct energy their way. This is no way to live. While you may not know how to release your judgment, trust that you *can*. This is where prayer comes in. The presence of a higher power can do for you what you cannot do for yourself. You can give over your discomfort to a presence beyond you and trust it's being taken care of.

Our true nature is love, but we forget that. We learn to turn our back on love and rely on judgment to keep us safe from all the separate people and experiences that we fear. But deep down, *we are love.* The role of our inner guide is to lead us toward feelings, thoughts, and situations that spark a remembrance of love, because when we recall love, we want more of it. Love has an invisible force field of positive energy that pulls us toward it. When we recognize that we're disconnected from love, we ask our inner guide for help and we'll once again be able to feel that pull instead of resisting it.

The practices in this step will help you remember your love nature. Upon remembering, you'll want more of it, and to access that love, you'll be called to give up judgment. You will see clearly how judgment blocks love and will want to clear whatever stands in the way of living in your truth. Following the practices in the next pages will help you invite the presence of your inner guide into your subconscious so that a spiritual intervention can unfold.

Let's begin to surrender a judgment you've been unwilling to address.

Name the judgment here:

_____

PRAY TO RELEASE YOUR JUDGMENT

It's time to take judgment off the altar and replace it with love. The profound act of surrendering your fear and judgment to the care of your inner guide will change the way you live. When you come to accept that you can transcend negativity whenever you choose, you'll begin to know a new form of freedom and happiness. You begin a dialogue with the nonphysical support that is always available to you. But you cannot access this guidance without inviting it in, so when you pray, you invite the presence of love into your consciousness. To help you establish a prayer practice of your own, I've offered some of my favorite prayers. You may find that one prayer in particular resonates with you.

When you pray, you send an invitation to spirit to help you restore your judgmental thoughts back to love. Spirit is the voice of our right-minded self; it's where we turn when we feel caught up in fear and judgment. When we pray to spirit, we ask for help to undo our mind's decision to judge. As we become aware of our judgmental thoughts, we must return to our decision-making mind and choose again through prayer.

We don't have to ask for help regarding specific problems. As I mentioned earlier, you shouldn't. For instance, don't go to spirit with questions like whether you should take a certain job or leave a certain relationship or which car to purchase. To do so would be a misunderstanding of how we are meant to ask spirit for help. When we ask for specific help (which boy, which car, and so forth), we're arrogantly assuming that we know what the problem is and then demanding that spirit answer us in the form that we have set up. Most of the time, though, we have yet to discover the root cause of the problem. Asking spirit to answer a specific but ultimately incorrect question is of no help. Therefore, instead of praying for a specific outcome, we must ask spirit to help us return our thoughts back to love. The secret to prayer is to forget what we think we need and surrender to spiritual guidance instead.

If you're new to prayer, don't judge the practice. Remember that this book is about stepping outside your comfort zone. If you're going to give up a destructive pattern that has held you back for years, you must be willing to try something new. So don't get hung up about this prayer practice—just do it. The words don't matter. Nor does it matter whether you pray to God, the Universe, or your inner guide. Your intention to transform fear into love is what creates the miracle. To help you get into the practice of praying, I've recorded a prayer for you to listen to. Visit GabbyBernstein .com/bookresources for my audio recording.

A Prayer for Surrender

Releasing judgment requires spiritual surrender. Without your sincere desire to let go, you'll struggle to give over your judgment and invite spirit in. Spiritual guidance is available to you all the time. You just need to turn over your judgment to receive it. This prayer will help you do just that. It is a simple and powerful way to begin your practice of communicating with your inner guide.

> *Dear inner guide, I need help with my judgment*
> *toward _____. I'm ready to surrender this now. I*
> *welcome in the presence of love to guide me back to*
> *truth and grace. I'm ready to release this judgment*
> *and see through the eyes of love.*

This prayer is perfect if you're feeling stuck and resistant toward releasing your judgment. Use the surrender prayer to enter a new energetic state that supports your desire to be free from attack thoughts. This is a practice in letting go and allowing.

A Prayer for Acceptance

In the Twelve Steps of Alcoholics Anonymous they say that carrying a resentment is like taking a bat and hitting yourself over the head with it. Take that in and think about how your judgment makes you feel. Maybe you feel high and justified for a few minutes, but that self-righteous satisfaction wears off. In fact, judgment lowers your energy, hinders your recovery, and keeps you stuck in a low vibe. This prayer will help you accept that your judgment no longer serves you.

The acceptance prayer has helped me see through the lens of love whenever fear has me in a headlock, and I turn to this prayer whenever my judgment has gotten the best of me. I trust that it will always remind me that what I'm judging is not what I think it is. Through the energy of acceptance I release my grievances and accept a solution of the highest good. Enjoy this acceptance prayer from the Big Book of Alcoholics Anonymous:

Acceptance is the answer to all my problems today.
When I am disturbed, it is because I find some
person, place, thing, or situation—some fact of my
life—unacceptable to me, and I can find no serenity

until I accept that person, place, thing, or situation as being exactly the way it is supposed to be at this moment.

This prayer has a powerful energy behind it. Even if acceptance feels way out of reach, saying the words of this prayer will change your attitude. Practice this prayer regularly and pay attention to your internal shifts.

A Prayer to Choose Again

Lesson 243 of *A Course in Miracles* offers this affirmation: "Today I will judge nothing that occurs." I use this message from the *Course* as a daily prayer to help me choose to release my judgment. It is a powerful way to begin your day: Judgment is a choice you make, and when you align your mind with the choice to release judgment, you will be guided to do so. Practice using this prayer in the morning when you wake up. The moment you open your eyes, recite, "Today I will judge nothing that occurs." Pay close attention to how the rest of your day flows. You may be quicker to catch yourself in a judgmental thought or you may stop yourself from saying something judgmental and choose another topic instead.

Today I will judge nothing that occurs.

These seven words are profound. When you say this prayer, you consciously choose to realign your thoughts with love and let the voice of your inner guide lead the way. The more you make this choice, the less you will judge. In time this prayer will become second nature; it will be an easy solution to all your judgments. I love this practice because it keeps me committed.

If this prayer resonates with you, then set it as an alarm to go off on your phone throughout the day, and trust that spirit will intervene throughout your day to restore your thoughts back to love.

A Prayer to Forgive Your Thoughts

The final prayer is to forgive the thought. Whenever we have a judgmental thought, we can erase it through forgiveness. I've gotten into the practice of witnessing my judgmental thoughts and quickly forgiving them. I silently say to myself:

I forgive this thought and I choose again.

This prayer offers me immediate relief. In an instant I can end the judgment cycle through the power of my intentions. When I intend to forgive the thought, I pardon myself for choosing wrongly and I realign with my right mind. In any moment I can find forgiveness through my practice. The moment you choose to forgive your thought, you realign with love and forgiveness is bestowed upon you.

Forgiveness is a practice because it is ongoing. I find that I have to forgive my thoughts all throughout the day. The ego voice of judgment is always at the forefront of our minds, so we have to lean on forgiveness to reprogram our thinking and restore our thoughts back to love.

Throughout the day, pay close attention to your judgments and use the prayer practice of forgiving a thought to bring you back to grace. You can do it silently anywhere, anytime. All you have to do is choose it.

HOW TO USE THE PRAYERS

I handpicked these four prayers specifically to help you release judgment and invite spiritual guidance. Choose at least one of these and begin to practice it regularly. The more you get into conscious contact with a higher power, the more support and guidance you'll receive. Know that there's no right or wrong way to pray—a prayer can come through your spoken word or your thoughts and intentions. I find it very powerful to put pen to paper and write my prayers in my journal. When I write them down, I feel like I'm releasing my internal suffering and inviting an invisible force to heal me. There's a special place in Step 3 of your Judgment Detox journal for you to write down your prayers. If writing your prayers feels good to you, make it part of your daily spiritual practice. Just begin to replace your judgment with prayer and let your inner guide lead the way.

My hope is that prayer becomes a daily practice for you. When you pray, you tune in to the energy of love, your true essence, your source. The more you surrender to that source, the more momentum you will feel behind you. The energy of love will propel you forward and attract what you desire. As you continue on your journey of clearing judgment, you'll need the energy of love as your guide. Each new prayer will clear the path, and when you pray for help, you always receive guidance.

PAY ATTENTION TO THE GUIDANCE YOU RECEIVE

The next part of Step 3 is to pay attention to the guidance you receive. While everyone has the ability to interact with spiritual guidance, we connect in our own unique ways. When you pray, you'll receive guidance in ways that resonate with you and reflect your belief systems. You get to interpret spiritual guidance in whatever form comes naturally to you. For instance, I consider myself to be claircognizant, which means that when I pray, I often receive guidance as a sense of knowing something on a gut level. A thought will randomly enter my mind, and while I don't know why it showed up, I trust it nonetheless. When I feel that sense of trust, I know that it is coming from a nonphysical divine source. So when I say a prayer, I expect that the guidance I'll receive will come as a sense of knowing. I've often described this as the sense of an authoritative inner voice directing me. It's a strong sensation that I cannot deny, like when I heard my inner voice direct me to turn on the television, guiding me to Joel Osteen's sermon.

Spiritual guidance comes in creative forms. Throughout the years I've met countless people who have told me that they found my work because my book literally fell off a shelf in front of them. These folks all describe a similar story of how they were consciously or unconsciously praying for change, which led them to the self-help section of the bookstore. Then one of my books fell off the shelf onto their feet. I always respond, "You read it when you need it." Spirit works in creative ways, so it's not uncommon to be led to a book, teacher, YouTube video, documentary, or class that is meant to help guide your spiritual development.

Most of the guidance you receive will be designed to help you learn, grow, and heal over time. While sometimes guidance can instantly resolve a conflict, most of the time you're being guided to a person, situation, or lesson that will help you heal the root cause of the issue. Remember, true relief from judgment and separation comes when we heal the dark beliefs that dwell beneath them. That's why we're often guided to exactly what we need to heal the spiritual condition.

We all think we want a quick fix and instant relief, but our inner wisdom knows that what we really want is to return to love. The only way to truly restore our faith in love is to be willing to heal. We must say yes to the guidance we receive and follow the direction to show up for our wounds. For instance, maybe you judge your parents for not taking care of you as a child. When you surrender and pray for guidance, the next day you may see an interview in a magazine with a therapist who specializes in childhood neglect. You then look up this therapist online and find out that her practice is only blocks from where you live. Within a week you have your first session lined up and you feel safe exploring your childhood wounds because you've been guided to a doctor who can help. This is one of the ways that spiritual guidance works. You accept that you've chosen fear over love. You pray for help. You receive guidance that will help you change your mind. And then you follow the guidance you receive to return to love.

One story that beautifully illustrates this comes from my friend Katie. In 2010 Katie lost her second job in two years and was exhausted and frustrated by the recession. She felt totally defeated and ashamed at being jobless once again. She wasn't a particularly spiritual person at the time, but in the midst of so much fear and uncertainty, she decided to pray—to what or whom she wasn't even sure. But she prayed to see the situation differently, and she surrendered to whatever came up for her. Instantly she felt a weight lift and received a clear message in the form of an intuitive knowing: Her dream career *was* available to her if she was willing to be patient and creative. She immediately quit applying for jobs that didn't excite her. She focused her energy on being open to what did. And within a few weeks, a dear friend of hers put her in touch with . . . me! I was looking for a new copy editor for some freelance work, and a mutual friend of ours recommended Katie. At the time Katie thought she needed a full-time job, but she listened to the guidance she received and said yes to this unexpected offer. She is now a successful self-employed writer and editor (who prays regularly!). She even helped edit this book!

This is one of the ways that spiritual guidance works. You accept that you've chosen fear over love. You pray for help. You receive guidance that will help you change your mind. And then you follow the guidance you receive to return to love.

When you begin your prayer practice, pay attention to

how you receive your communication from spirit. The more faith you put behind your intuitive connection, the more guidance you will receive. Take note of the way spirit speaks to you and trust what's coming through.

You may have past experiences of receiving guidance that you can now lean on to help develop your faith. I call this spiritual proof. Whenever we have a moment of supportive synchronicity, we are being led by spirit. Take a moment to think about any times in your life where you've received nonphysical guidance.

Write down those examples in your journal now.

Take a moment to honor this spiritual proof and allow it to give you momentum as you strengthen your spiritual connection through prayer. If you haven't ever received spiritual proof, get psyched—the prayers in this book will open up your consciousness to receive intuitive guidance. That's what this step is designed for, so let's get started!

Perhaps your spiritual guidance comes through people. You may get the exact message you need from a stranger on the street or through an inspirational quote you see on Instagram. You can even receive guidance in a dream, especially if you pray before you go to sleep. If you say any one of the four prayers before you fall asleep, you'll guide your dreams to help you resolve negativity and judgment. When you pray, you can find healing guidance everywhere.

I also find comfort in the fact that prayer isn't just about our individual needs. Our prayers are felt by others too. When you send loving prayers to others, they can energetically sense it. Your prayers have an energy frequency that can be felt from a distance. If you've been judging people, you've been sending them a prayer of negativity. To help you transform this energy transmission from negative to positive, proactively shift from judgment to a prayer for love. Prayer can release your grievances and clear space for healing in relationships once based on fear. For instance, early in my career I had a business associate with whom I worked very closely. We were in our early twenties and very ego driven. Our relationship was based on separation, comparison, and judgment. There was serious tension between us and we couldn't find resolution. We needed a miracle! I ultimately became so fed up with the negativity between us that I asked a spiritual mentor for advice on healing the relationship. She said, "Pray for her to have the happiness and peace you want for yourself." Wow, this totally surprised me. "Um, why would I pray for her? She's the one who makes me crazy," I said. My mentor explained that by praying for her, I'd release my judgment and feel better. When I felt better, I'd release my energetic attack on her and she'd feel released too.

I was willing to do whatever it took to heal this relationship, so I began to pray for her daily. I prayed for her to be happy, successful, and at peace. I prayed for her to have all the joy and serenity that I wanted for myself. And even though I was skeptical, it worked. I started feeling better pretty much right away. The love within me was stronger than my ego's judgment. Praying for her reconnected me to my truth and it felt awesome to let go of my grievance. But the coolest part of this experience was that she felt my shift too. Within a week of my prayer practice she started acting differently—she was kinder, more compassionate, and just more fun to be around. I know that my prayers shifted the energy between us. Prayer helped me release my energetic attack on her, and in that release, she felt free to be more loving toward me. It was the miracle we needed, and in time we healed our relationship.

A *Course in Miracles* teaches that "prayer is the medium of miracles." When we pray we shift our perception from fear to love. A prayer is a spiritual invitation for a mental cleansing—we wash away the ego's perception of attack and shift into a remembrance of love. By praying for my friend to have the same happiness and peace I wanted for myself, I let go of my ego's perception and let love restore my mind.

Miraculous shifts await you in this practice. Begin by reciting one of the prayers above every day. Let your prayers restore your thoughts back to love. By praying daily you can be led to situations that will guide you to change your perception about your judgments. I like to begin my day with a prayer because I commit to love from the onset. But you can also pray all throughout the day and receive support as you need it.

There are countless ways that prayer will serve you. As you begin your daily prayer practice, pay attention to what comes through for you. Most important, don't question the loving messages you receive. Resistance to love keeps you stuck in the judgment cycle, while prayer releases that resistance. Remember, these messages and guidance are simply leading your thoughts back to love. Surrender to the guidance and let love in.

Once you receive the guidance you can elect either to follow it or to ignore it. It's important to know that spirit won't give you anything that you can't handle. Your inner guide is always leading you to what is of the highest good for you and for all. So have faith in this inner wisdom and fearlessly follow the lead. You'll be amazed by the weight that's lifted simply by saying yes to the spiritual guidance that is presented to you.

While you are free to ignore the guidance you receive, doing so may cause you to unconsciously judge yourself more. You'll feel in some way as though you're denying your truth. This can spin you into more shame and guilt, which will perpetuate the judgment cycle. I mention this not to alarm you but to make you aware of what can happen when you repress the voice of your inner guide. Remember that this is a practice of returning to your truth. The intuition you receive is only guiding you back to your right mind of love. Trust this and you'll be compelled to listen and follow the guidance you receive.

I made prayer the third step of the Judgment Detox because I wanted to give you a tool that would support you in the work to come. Begin to rely on prayer as your guide back to love. There is nothing more powerful than releasing the need to control and relying on a power greater than you to restore your thoughts and energy. When you loosen your grip and let spirit lead the way, your life will become a happy dream.

Prayer practice seamlessly guides you to the next step. When we pray, we can suspend time and release the past. The profound act of surrendering the past through prayer can help you see someone in their holiness no matter what they've done to you. This radical act of seeing someone with acceptance, love, and compassion is the message behind Step 4 in the Judgment Detox.

As we build upon previous lessons, remain willing to heal your judgment and you'll be led to release more resistance each day. Remember that this is a process and celebrate the miracles along the way by documenting them in your journal. There is no need to aim for a major breakthrough. Add up each miracle moment, and when you're done, you'll look back and be amazed by the shifts.

See for the First Time

For many years I struggled with my relationship to my father. We disagreed on some important issues, which created a lot of tension. Every phone call (and we had them weekly) would end with a heated argument. The separation between us got worse as the years went by.

But once I became more aware of my judgmental ways, something changed. One Sunday afternoon I received my weekly call from my dad. We were civil for about fifteen minutes before we began arguing about the same old stuff. We raised our voices and fell right back into our pattern of attack and separation. As I practically yelled into my phone, I suddenly witnessed myself reverting back to childish behavior. So I did something different: I got silent and let him speak. In the silence he was able to calm down and tell me how he was feeling. "You know, Gabby," he said, "I feel very judged by you." I let his words settle in and I felt a moment of compassion. "Dad, you're right," I said. "I have been judging you. I'm sorry for that. It's something I'm working on." We apologized to each other and civilly ended the call.

That conversation gave me a valuable opportunity to see that while I felt justified in my anger, judgment wasn't the right response. By stepping outside the pattern of disagreement, I could see my part in the situation.

I felt guilty for my judgment. At the time, I was in the midst of writing a spiritual book about love, compassion, and oneness, and all the while I was deeply judging my own father. Witnessing this behavior was uncomfortable and brought up lots of complicated feelings, but I knew there was a spiritual solution—so I prayed to release my judgment toward my father. I didn't know how the judgment would be released, but I trusted that spirit had a plan to show me the way.

The following week my father asked my brother and me to accompany him to temple for my grandfather's yahrzeit, which in the Jewish faith marks the anniversary of a death. I hadn't set foot in my childhood temple in nearly a decade. While the interior had been redesigned, nothing about it really seemed to have changed. As was standard for us when I was growing up, we walked in late and had to shuffle through the last row to find seats. I enjoyed being back in my temple that night, and I felt a sense of calm come over me.

As the Universe would have it, the rabbi delivered a sermon on the value of letting go of judgment and the need for compassion toward others. His words resonated with me deeply and I paid close attention to the spiritual guidance I was receiving. At the end of the service the rabbi looked toward the back of the room and said, "There's a lovely family here tonight who have been members of this congregation for decades. I want to acknowledge the Bernsteins. Edgar Bernstein is here with his two children, Gabby and Max. I honor Edgar for his commitment to his parents, as he never misses either of their yahrzeits. This morning, in preparation for Edgar's father's yahrzeit, I went into the temple membership records from decades ago and pulled something special." The rabbi stood on the pulpit holding in his hand what he revealed to be my grandfather's temple membership card from more than sixty years ago. My grandfather had filled it out by hand, and in the column for additional members, he had inscribed the names of his two children, my father and aunt. The rabbi looked at my father and invited him up to the pulpit to give him the card.

Deeply moved by the rabbi's gesture, my father burst into tears. I looked at him crying at the end of the aisle and I gently scooted past my brother to give my dad a hug. This was a miraculous shift. In that moment my past resentment dissolved. I saw him as a devoted son, a proud father, and an honored member of his congregation. My judgment was transformed into love. I saw his innocence, his truth, and his light. I saw him for the first time.

The experience of seeing my father without his past, without our history, and without my resentment was one of the most healing moments of my life. In that holy instant my thoughts realigned with love and I remembered the truth of who we are: We are all spiritual beings who are love. When we can put aside our stories, pretense, and judgment, love can be restored. Seeing others for the first time means we see their innocence and oneness. We can recognize the light within them as the same light that shines within ourselves. In the presence of someone's light, judgment cannot live.

This is Step 4 in the Judgment Detox: See for the first time.

The steps leading up to this point have prepared you for this next phase of healing. You've witnessed your judgment without judgment, which has given you the willingness to start on the path. You've honored the wounds that live beneath the judgment, which has given you an opportunity to accept your past and choose again. And you offered your judgments to the care of your inner guide for transformation and guidance. You're now ready to receive the blessing of seeing the person you judge in their innocence and light.

The experience of seeing someone for the first time is one of deep relief. You free the person from the stories you've placed upon him or her and you free yourself from the bondage of attack. You'll feel relieved because you'll be returning to your truth. When you see someone you've judged through the light of love rather than the lens of darkness, you will experience a miracle: You shift from body identification to spirit identification. When you recognize someone solely as a body—a physical being—you can place your fear-based stories onto them. You project onto them and you expect them to behave a certain way. But when you release those projections and have the experience of seeing them as spirit, all those stories disappear. If even for an instant you let down your guard and choose to see through the lens of love rather than fear, you will be one step closer to freedom. That instant is enough to activate energetic momentum that will greatly speed up your healing.

The thought of seeing for the first time without guilt and judgment may trigger you. Your ego desperately wants to hold on to the belief that it's unsafe to let go of your judgment. But the stories, beliefs, and energy you've put into judging others have become, however inadvertently, a defense against love. If you sense your own resistance to this step, simply pray for your inner guide to heal it. You have powerful tools now and can use them to propel you forward, toward freedom from judgment. Your prayers will help you release the ego's resistance and surrender to the process.

Seeing someone for the first time requires spiritual surrender. This practice is not logical, it's experiential. Trust that your intentions to see through the lens of love are enough for you to experience a miracle. Follow my guidance, release the outcome, and allow this step to unfold naturally.

THE PATHWAY TO SEE
FOR THE FIRST TIME

To begin the practice of seeing someone for the first time, you must start by accepting them where they are. It's a myth to think that you'll feel better after they change their behavior. In order to see them in innocence, you must accept them exactly where they are.

Acceptance

The most loving thing we can do for someone is to accept them. The most unloving thing we can do is try to change them. When you try to change someone, you're effectively saying that you know what is best for them. Your unsolicited "help" is a way of controlling and judging them. People may not show up the way you want them to, but when you accept them where they are, you can let go, forgive, and release.

Now, it can be difficult to accept someone when we think they're making bad decisions. But like us, they too have a guidance system helping to navigate what's best for them. Importantly, we all have turning points in our lives that offer the gift of surrender. But if you try to "fix" someone else, you rob them of that opportunity. When we make ourselves responsible for another person's happiness, we can deprive them of the opportunity to hit bottom. So instead of trying to prevent them from hitting their knees, you can pray for their experience to be gentle and to come with clear guidance and support.

If someone wants to change and asks for your help, you can show up and offer support. But it's not helpful, kind, or loving to try to impose change on anyone. When we invite spirit in through prayer, we return to our right mind and find acceptance. A *Course in Miracles* teaches that spirit accepts and ego analyzes. Spirit accepts what is true, which is that we are all love.

The other person doesn't need correction from you. What needs correction is your mistaken decision to identify with ego instead of spirit. All the judgment in our mind stems from that mistaken choice to perceive the ego's world of separation and attack. When we see through the perception of our body rather than the perception of our spirit, judgment is inevitable. In Step 3, you began to establish a spiritual connection as you understand it. That practice is required of you now, because you must rely on spirit to see someone for the first time and be guided toward acceptance.

Accepting someone where they are is not only the kindest thing you can do for them, it's also the kindest thing you can do for yourself. It's important to understand what judgment does to you on a metaphysical level. The spiritual medium Esther Hicks and her guides, collectively called Abraham, say:

> *Everyone holds a mix of opinions, beliefs, and expectations on a myriad of subjects. When you give your attention to something, that Vibration becomes acti-*

vated and comes to the forefront. And the more often you focus upon it, and cause it to come to the forefront, the more dominant it becomes.

You have the option of making a good-feeling aspect of another person dominant in your Vibration or of making a bad-feeling aspect dominant, and whatever aspect you regularly choose will become the Vibrational basis of your relationship. When your happiness becomes your highest priority, and so you deliberately keep active the best-feeling aspects of others, you will train your Vibrational frequency in such a way that they will not be able to rendezvous with you in any way that does not feel good when it happens.

The only way for anyone to be consistently happy is to understand that the feeling of happiness is simply about alignment with the Source within.

What you focus on, you create. By consistently practicing to accept someone where they are and see them with compassion, you realign with your true love nature. Through acceptance you release the resistance you've placed within your relationship, clearing the way for healing and for you to access more loving thoughts and feelings. When you change your thoughts and feelings about another person, you change your energy toward them. The other person will receive your shift in energy and feel released by you. Best of all, your shift in energy gives you momentum to continue releasing judgment so you can feel complete and free. Acceptance offers you this freedom.

Accept Yourself

Self-acceptance has the power to completely reorganize your experience of yourself and life. When you look at your list of judgmental targets, is your name at or near the top? If so, practicing self-acceptance is essential to healing your relationship to yourself and aligning with love.

My friend Sam is a wonderful example of what practicing self-acceptance can do. He struggled for a few years trying to find his confidence in his career. He'd left corporate America to become an entrepreneur, but was having trouble gaining momentum. He started project after project, only to see each one fizzle out and fail. Finally, Sam saw an opportunity to get involved in a big deal that he thought could be really successful. Like his other projects, however, pretty quickly things started going south. Not only was he working ridiculous hours to try to save the deal, but he feared he would lose all the money he'd invested in it. The months he put into the project felt like years, and when the dust settled, he had nothing to show for it. Understandably, it was an incredibly dark time for him.

Sam found himself at a crossroad. He could turn to self-judgment and attack. He could believe all the stories he'd been telling himself about how it's too hard to be an entrepreneur and how he just wasn't cut out for it. Or he could choose differently. He could instead choose to accept his past and honor the hard work and education he'd gotten out of taking risks. Through self-acceptance he could redirect his focus from what he hadn't accomplished and onto what he had learned. Miraculously, and through a little guidance and a lot of self-love, Sam chose acceptance.

In the right-minded headspace of self-acceptance, Sam saw himself for the first time. He let go of his stories from the past and embraced the man he was in the present. He chose to celebrate his growth and his willingness. He even celebrated his mistakes as valuable guidance for the future. Sam's act of self-acceptance gave him energy, enthusiasm, and excitement for what was coming. Acceptance made him feel creative and cleared space for intuitive ideas to come forward. Because he was aligned with the energy of love, he could hear the voice of spirit guide him.

Shortly after Sam chose to accept himself, the miracles started rolling in. In the space of self-acceptance, Sam had released all resistance. In the absence of resistance, inspiration flowed to him freely. One afternoon Sam happened onto a creative business idea, one that, as far as he could tell, no one else was doing and that could be acted on right away. It was the opportunity he'd been waiting for. Because Sam had released his self-judgment and aligned with love, he had the energy to put things into motion immediately. Very quickly, Sam's idea became a six-figure business that now supports his family and has endless room for growth. Sam could have gone one of two ways in his career. Through the power of acceptance he chose the right direction.

I share Sam's story to inspire you to see the power of acceptance when it comes to both ourselves and others. When we accept others we give them space to grow. When we accept ourselves, we clear the path to create a new story. Marianne Williamson says, "Let go of your story so the Universe can write a new one for you." The moment you choose acceptance, you invite the Universe to start writing.

Exercise in Acceptance

Begin your practice of acceptance by revisiting your list of judgments from Step 1. Pick one from the list that is still triggering you, even after the EFT and prayer. Maybe you're afraid to release a judgment toward a person who's harmed you or maybe you're afraid of what will happen if you stop judging yourself. Choose a judgment that you're ready to release and bring it to your practice now.

At the top of your journal write the name of the person you've judged. (Maybe it's your own name!)

Next to the name, write a list of all the aspects of this person that you like. If they're someone who has seriously hurt you, it may be hard to find any positive qualities. In that case, focus on the lessons you've learned from the relationship. Even in the worst situations or relationships, there are always spiritual opportunities for growth and healing. You can focus on your growth and learning as a result of an otherwise negative situation. You can direct your attention to how this person has given you an opportunity to practice the Judgment Detox. Or you can choose to see this person with compassion, accepting that a happy person wouldn't treat someone so poorly. This process of redirecting your focus from judgment to acceptance requires your willingness to reach for simple, better-feeling thoughts. Even moving from the thought *I hate you* to *I accept that you are unwell* can shift your energy around the relationship. Slowly reach for ways to accept, and witness your energy shift along the way. I've witnessed many of my audience members publicly share terrifying stories of how they'd been abused, attacked, or shamed, and through the recovery process they found their spiritual connection and redirected the course of their lives. Even if they were unwilling to truly forgive their perpetrators right away, they could see how the trauma was the catalyst for great spiritual growth. If you're struggling to find something you like about the person whom you've judged, try to focus on the lessons you've learned from the relationship. As you generate the list, proactively direct your focus to what you appreciate about this person, even if you can conjure up only one thing.

As you read through your list, check in with how you feel as you direct your focus from the negative to the appreciation for the positive. See if you feel more accepting of the person now that you've shifted away from what you wish you could change and onto what is good about them (or what lessons you've learned as a result of your relationship or interaction with them). Take notes in your journal about how you feel. Maybe you feel relief in letting go of trying to change someone who can't be changed. Or maybe you feel compassion and love toward them. It's possible that this practice may make you feel defensive. This is just your ego holding on to judgment and trying to keep you stuck in the dark. If you resist the feeling of love, continue to focus your attention on the good that has come from this situation. By subtly shifting your focus, you can get closer to acceptance. The more you shift your focus to acceptance, the more relief you will feel.

Recognize the Other Person Is You

The greatest way to see someone's innocence is to recognize that it's your own. We all have the same problem and the same solution. Our problem is that we chose to detour into the wrong mind of judgment. The solution is to choose love instead. And in our hearts, we share the same desires: We all want to be happy, healthy, and free. We all want to be loved. Accepting our oneness with others helps us recognize ourselves in them.

The great Kundalini yoga master Yogi Bhajan left behind five sutras for the Aquarian Age, one of which was "Recognize the other person is you." Yogi Bhajan had prophesied the state of the world that we would be living in today. He could see the division and separation, and he knew that we'd need to call on more oneness in order to survive. He could see that the root cause of our worldly problems would continue to stem from separation, and he instilled in his students, readers, and audiences that we must recognize the other person is us. To dissolve the separation of our times we must live by this sutra.

I've had many opportunities to put this sutra into practice. One example happened when I was renting a car. I was traveling for work and rushing to get from the airport to my meeting. I was already running late, so it wasn't helping that I walked into a long line at the rental counter. I stood patiently for fifteen minutes (about all the patience I had), and once I reached the register I was eager to grab my keys and go. The woman at the counter could sense my controlling energy the moment I walked up to her register. I said in a curt tone, "I'm in a really big rush and I'd love to get the car as soon as possible." She looked at me and laughed. "It's gonna take as long as it needs to," she said. At this point I knew I was in trouble. I said under my breath, "Well, you better hurry up."

My negative vibe did not make her work faster. In fact, my attitude totally pissed her off. She walked away from the register for no apparent reason only to return five minutes later with no explanation, and she took forever to put my information into the system. Her power play sent me into a tizzy. I started sweating and looking around to see if I could find her manager. I then rudely asked for her name and threatened to call the corporate offices and complain. Not surprisingly, this didn't help. My negativity only fueled hers. Our altercation turned into a heated argument and her manager came over to scold me for raising my voice. Needless to say, it was not my brightest moment.

I finally got behind the wheel, already thirty minutes late for my meeting, sweating and pissed off. Then I got stuck in traffic. This only made me even more upset. I started blaming the woman and replaying the situation over and over in my mind, my anger escalating to an all-time high. I was driving unsafely and sounding the horn any time someone cut me off. I was in bad shape. But I had an important meeting that I was already late for and I really needed to pull myself together. So I said a prayer, asking for a shift in my perception. Within moments I heard Yogi Bhajan's voice echoing in my consciousness: "Recognize the other person is you." My immediate response to this guidance was "What! How is she me?"

I took a deep breath and let the message sink in. Then I looked closely at the situation and became willing to see it differently. I chose to see what it was about this woman that triggered me to such a degree. In a few minutes of reflection

I came to accept that she and I had a lot in common. We were both trying to access our power in the situation. We both wanted to be in control and wield authority. My need to be in control was her need to be in control. My need to feel power was hers. In an instant I could recognize her wounds as my own and see her for the first time.

Sitting in a car stuck in a traffic jam, now nearly an hour late, I began to cry tears of relief. I cried for the divine spiritual assignment that was presented to me. I cried for the miraculous shift of recognizing the other person was me. I cried for the opportunity to truly experience Yogi Bhajan's sutra. This message was no longer a catchphrase—it was a huge step in my spiritual development and healing.

You can begin to bring this sutra into your own life by choosing to see people for the truth of who they are and not for the projections you've placed on them. Practice seeing their innocence by honoring all that they've been through and the challenges they've faced, even if you have no idea what those challenges may be. Your acceptance list will help you redirect your focus to see them in their light.

Then recognize that this person is you. To truly honor another human being, you must recognize that the darkness you see in them is a disowned part of your own shadow. When you judge the shadows in others, you're merely projecting what you've denied within yourself. Whenever you're triggered by others, it's because they're mirroring back elements of your shadow that you're unwilling to heal. Turn your judgment into gratitude. Thank them for being a reflection and giving you the opportunity to continue to learn and grow on your spiritual path. See them as your teacher showing you your universal curriculum. Recognize that they are you.

See Them in Light

My late mentor and friend Dr. Wayne Dyer said, "See the light in others and treat them as if that is all you see." Wayne truly embodied this belief system, and I think it's the reason for how joyful and happy he was. That happiness is available to all of us when we bring this message into our daily practice. The next time you walk into your office ready to judge your coworkers, or the next time you turn on the news ready to judge our current affairs, say this prayer: "The light in you is all I see." You can recite this prayer whenever you've made a judgment of anyone. Bring it to the relationships that hold the greatest separation for you—the people whom you've made special and better than you and people whom you've perceived as less than or even hateful. Unless we work at it, we will judge everyone in our lives—from strangers we have brief encounters with to our closest loved ones, children, parents, and spouses. Whenever you notice yourself judging someone, say silently to yourself, "The light in you is all I see."

Go about your day paying attention to the thoughts you have about others. Witness yourself when an attack thought comes up, and witness when you've made someone special or separate. Acknowledge an attack thought and a special thought as one and the same: judgment. Apply Step 1 and witness your judgment without judgment. The moment you witness your judgmental nature, just say your prayer: "The light in you is all I see."

Early in my career, this was a tool I gave to my students. I told them to go out into the streets of New York City, silently repeating "The light in you is all I see" at each encounter. They used it on the subway, in the deli, at work with their coworkers, and in their homes with family and friends. At every encounter, they were reminding themselves to see only the light in others. I asked them to carry on like this for one full week and return to the group to share their experiences.

The results were amazing. Each woman came back with her own miracle to share. Some shared that their formerly standoffish coworkers were acting kinder. Others said they resolved issues with their partners that had been plaguing them for several years. Some women even shared that they felt depression lift and joy settle in. When you go out of your way to see people in their light, you are returning to truth. It can transform your life quickly. You feel relief in letting people off the hook. The simple truth is that it just feels better to be accepting and compassionate. It feels empowering to see love wherever you are. Yogi Bhajan said, "If you can't see God in all, you can't see God at all."

When your only job is to see everyone in light, you have no time to focus on fault and judgment. We spend our days living in the judgment cycle, and the moment you get yourself out of it, you clear space to receive a stream of well-being and joy. Esther Hicks and Abraham say, "There is only a stream of well-being that flows. You can allow it or resist it, but it flows just the same." When you proactively see others in light, you allow the stream of well-being to flow. In the absence of your judgment, all that's left is love.

The quickest pathway to living in the light is to recognize the light wherever you are. See the light in your terrifying, tyrannical boss. See the light in your cheating ex. See the light in the murderer on the news. I recognize this concept may trigger you. You may be thinking, *How can I see the light in a murderer? That's impossible.* It might even strike you as ridiculous or unnecessary. But when you accept that someone must be very sick and internally tortured or empty to do something so horrible, compassion can set in.

This is the final practice in this step: Call on compassion.

Practice Compassion

Compassion is the antidote to judgment. When you accept someone right where they are, you can see them for all their good *and* bad. When you recognize the other person is you, you see your reflection in their shadow and in their light. And when you choose to see them in light, love shines through. But even with these practices in your spiritual toolbox, you will waver and return to judgment. The ego is powerful and can suck you back into the stories of separation. You may also find that you're willing to apply these practices to people who are easy to release, but that when it comes to a violent criminal or someone who wields a lot of power, there's just no way.

This is where compassion comes into play. Cultivating a perception of compassion helps you see someone's innocence. You can see that their own inner terror turned them into a monster. The trauma and turmoil that must go on inside of anyone who can gravely harm another person is unfathomable for most of us. And if this is a person incapable of feeling empathy or love, you can feel compassion for their inability to feel such an important human emotion. Seeing them with compassion helps you see their hardship, pain, and deep suffering. Recognizing their suffering through compassion does not mean that you pardon their wrongs. But it does mean that on a spiritual level you release them. On this level, releasing them is how you release yourself from the terror they created. Holding on to your judgment creates more terror in your mind and perpetuates the judgment cycle.

The practice of compassion is a choice. You can choose in any moment to focus your attention on someone's wrongdoing or on what might have allowed them to behave in such a fashion. When you redirect your focus away from what has been done and onto the sickness that led them to do it, compassion can set in. Compassionately witnessing someone in their darkness gives them permission to step into the light.

Compassion is a practice that comes more easily for some of us. Regardless of how difficult it seems, remember that you don't need to logically understand it or perfect it overnight. All you need is a willingness. Bring your empathy to the table and let compassion lead your thoughts. Even for a brief moment you can feel relief.

Each person you encounter on your life's path offers you spiritual assignments to strengthen your faith in love. When you accept these relationships (and your relationship to yourself) as spiritual assignments to remember love, your perceived issues change. You no longer see your problems with others as lifelong struggles; instead, you see them as opportunities to strengthen your faith. The spiritual act of seeing someone for the first time is one of the greatest spiritual practices you can apply. It will give you immense relief and everlasting rewards. When you make the shift from judgment to oneness, you send an energy wave throughout the world that touches every single soul. The world is healed each time you recognize the light in another being. And in doing so, we can fulfill our purpose here on Earth: to be the light and see the light in others.

Any one of the practices in this step will release resistance and open up the floodgates of well-being. Practicing acceptance will help you let down your guard and drop your judgments. Recognizing the other person is you will help you see your part in the story and remind you of the other person's innocence. Praying to see the light in all will reconnect you to your brothers and sisters so that you can realign with the flow of the Universe. And practicing compassion will release you from the bondage of judgment.

Apply these interchangeably and you'll begin to experience the step of seeing for the first time. Each of these exercises will dissolve the barriers you've built up against the world and restore your true nature. Seeing others for the first time is a blessing you give yourself. Ultimately you set *yourself* free. You free yourself from the imprisonment of judgment and recalibrate your energy to live in harmony with the light of the world.

This step on your Judgment Detox journey is where intense shifts in your psyche begin to occur. You begin to see the world in a whole new way. You let the world off the hook and accept that we're all in it together. Accept that we all judge, but we all long for love too. Realize that if more people chose love, the world would be a safer, happier, and healthier place.

This book doesn't exist just to make you feel better and help you attract more of what you want. This book is designed to create a movement of lightworkers who will heal the world one loving thought at a time. I want to transform the inner beliefs of millions of people throughout the world so that we shift the energy of the planet. Accept that you are part of a movement. The collective conscious is far more powerful than you can imagine. When one or more people gather in the name of love, miracles occur. Let's continue to return our thoughts to love and change the world that we see.

Start today. Bridge your awareness onto acceptance and compassion. See through the lens of light and recognize the other person is you.

The steps leading up to this point are enough to create radical change in your life. But there are two more important steps to set you in full motion. In the next step, I will bring in the bedrock of all spiritual practice: meditation. Throughout Step 5 you will be guided to put your left brain's logic aside and embrace your right brain's creative capacity to see with spiritual sight. If you're new to meditation, this is the perfect place to start. I will offer several unique guided meditation practices to help you surrender even more.

A devoted meditation practice will change you on both the psychological and physical levels. Meditation can alter ancient patterns and reorganize your nervous system. The beautiful part of the next step is that you will begin to see all the other steps fall into place in the midst of your stillness. Prepare now by opening your heart to go deeper on your healing path. There is so much joy for you on the other side.

Cut the Cords

When it comes to dealing with conflicts among my friends, in general I've found this to be pretty easy. I tend to be really good at working things out and finding solutions without hostility or tension. But my glimmering track record recently came to an end after I had a huge falling out with a childhood friend.

I don't think this friend—let's call him Jack—meant to cause me any harm. And I'm sure Jack didn't realize that his behavior had triggered one of my core wounds. In fact I wasn't even prepared to articulate just how devastated I was by his actions. And since I lacked this bit of self-awareness, I went into protection mode. It took me more than three weeks to actually confront him. In the meantime, I spent hours replaying the situation in my mind and falling deeper into a victim mentality.

Finally, after three weeks of no contact, I mustered up a bit of courage and called him. But as soon as he picked up, I started in with my devastation at his actions. I lectured him on all the ways he'd hurt me and how wrong I thought he was. My words were defensive and backed with a nasty tone. I took my upset to another level by saying, "I can't believe you'd act like this." My attitude and words shocked him, especially because he didn't see any of it coming. And that actually marked the *real* negative turning point. The moment I went from explaining how hurt I felt to judging Jack for his behavior was the moment that my side of the story no longer mattered. There was no more space for me to express my honest feelings—because now Jack was on the defense. His tone changed and the conversation got heated. We hung up the phone in a great deal of distress.

I didn't immediately realize what I'd done. I felt so justified in my anger. Moreover, I even felt proud that I'd spoken up for myself. Weeks went by and I didn't hear from Jack. I continued to be angry as I added fuel to my judgmental story. I played it out over and over in my mind, making myself right for how I acted. But the more angry and judgmental I became, the more upset I felt. It was a vicious cycle.

It seemed like we wouldn't be able to fix what was broken, that a lifelong friendship now had to dissolve. I accepted the "fate" of the situation—but even though I couldn't admit it, I felt an unconscious sense that it was all my fault. I knew deep down that nothing could justify the judgment and separation I'd placed on him. My judgment had done some serious damage.

As time went on, I thought of all the ways I could've handled the situation differently. How could I have been kinder and more loving? How could I truthfully share my feelings without judging? But obsessing about the past wasn't going to help me move forward. It was just keeping me stuck in a nightmarish cycle. I knew I had to bring the issue to my Judgment Detox practice. So I witnessed my judgment without judgment and I honored my wound and tapped on it. I prayed for spirit to intervene and I chose to see my friend as love and light.

All these practices helped soften my judgment. But there was another step I needed to take in order to mend the relationship on an energetic level. I needed to bring the judgment to my meditation practice for a spiritual cleanse. I couldn't call my friend and fix the situation over the phone, but I could clear the energy through my meditation. So I got comfortable on my pillow and began the next step in the Judgment Detox.

Before I meditated, I set the intention to heal the bond between us. I asked spirit to intervene and repair our energetic connection. I surrendered the relationship to my inner guide and asked for help. And within seconds I intuitively heard the voice of my inner guide say, "Send him love." The message felt soothing. I understood that it was time to heal the negativity between us through the energy of love. I listened to this guidance and began to send deep love to Jack through my meditation. In my mind's eye I saw myself hugging him closely. I felt his presence in the room. I let my mind wander toward all the qualities I loved about him as I began to cry. In that moment I felt as though time and space didn't exist. The past was dissolved and the future was nonexistent. The bond between us was restored through prayer and meditation. I felt lighter and more deeply connected to him than I ever had previously.

When I felt calm, I came out of my meditation. A few minutes after opening my eyes, I checked my phone to see what time it was, and I noticed a text message pop up. It was from Jack! He said, "I feel like it's time to resolve this." I sighed with relief and thanked the Universe for this guidance. The moment I released my judgment, he felt me let go and knew it was time to heal. That is the power of meditation.

Meditation has the capacity to transform all your relationships, including your relationship to yourself. When you tune in to the energy of love through your meditation practice, you invite an invisible force of love to take over. In the presence of that love, the past can fade away and the energetic cords of judgment can dissolve. We all have energetic cords binding us to people all over the world. Sometimes we have cord connections to people we don't even know. When you have a relationship with someone, your energy becomes connected, especially when a strong emotional event occurs between you. Energy cords can also be created when we make a contract or promise to someone, whether a business deal or a marriage or something less formal. Even when that relationship ends, the energy cord can still be intact, particularly in situations where you're thinking negative, judgmental thoughts about that person. Your judgment creates a cord that binds you to them whether you like it or not.

Even when you think a relationship is over, you will still feel the pain and drama that went on when you were "together." The cords of energy keep the drama going even when you're apart, and those strong energetic ties can make you feel drained, tired, and even upset. That's why it can be so hard to stop thinking about an ex-lover or stop obsessing about a business relationship that turned sour. This is what happened with my friend Jack. Even though we were physically separated and weren't speaking, I continued to feel resentful, angry, and shaken up because of the cord attachment. Physical separation was not enough to end a negative connection—it needed to be cleared on a spiritual level.

When you have a cord attachment to someone you've judged, you're stuck in a low-frequency relationship, playing out the drama over and over again. And that negativity goes beyond that one relationship: Your own energetic frequencies put out a lower vibration, attracting other relationships that represent the same judgment, separation, and negativity. Everything gets tangled up fast.

The good news is that you can heal your cord attachments through meditation. Even one meditation can cut a cord, release an energetic bond, and break the judgment cycle. This practice is the most important step for resolving past relationships and moving forward with grace. In order to move forward in new relationships and relieve yourself of the judgment and drama, you must cut the cords.

This step in the Judgment Detox helps you free yourself from the cycle of separation. Every step thus far has prepared you mentally and spiritually to dissolve any discomfort or destructive attachment. Now it's time to meditate. I've outlined six meditations that will help you energetically clear your judgmental attachments and heal. *Each meditation builds upon the next, so do one per day for the next six days.* Practice each meditation when you wake up in the morning. The goal is to reorganize your energy immediately and then pay attention to the miraculous shifts throughout the day.

I expect you to find major relief from these practices. One meditation may resonate with you more than another, but be sure to try them all in the order I've presented. Then once you've finished the six-day period, you can begin to use them interchangeably throughout your Judgment Detox. If you follow these six meditations over six days, you'll be able to clear the energetic ties that keep you bound to the pattern of judgment. These meditations will set you free and clear space for the final step in the Judgment Detox.

Day 1

Let's begin with the Cord-Cutting Meditation. It sends a powerful message to the Universe that you're ready to let go of the pattern of judgment and improve your psyche. (Visit GabbyBernstein.com/bookresources to get the audio recording of this meditation.) Follow my guidance and have your notebook by your side in case inspired ideas come forth throughout your meditation practice.

Day 1 Morning Meditation: Cord-Cutting Meditation

Sit comfortably cross-legged on the floor or in a chair.

Gently roll your shoulders back.

Take a deep breath in through your nose and breathe out through your mouth.

Breathe in.

Breathe out.

Breathe in.

Breathe out.

With each breath you'll begin to relax more and more.

Breathe in.

Breathe out.

Continue to focus on this cycle of breath.

Breathing in through your nose and out through your mouth.

Allow your thoughts to still and feel a sense of calm radiate through you as you prepare for deeper healing.

Invite the person whom you've been judging into your meditation now.

See them in your mind's eye, standing before you.

Allow yourself to feel any feelings of anger or resentment.

Be present with your feelings as you breathe.

Breathe in and breathe out.

Breathe into the discomfort that arises from seeing this person standing before you.

And breathe out.

Breathe in the feeling and release it.

See the thick, dark cord between you both.

Where is this cord attached? At your chest, your throat, your stomach?

Trust whatever image comes to your mind.

See the cord clearly and prepare to cut it.

Prepare to detach yourself from the negative energy of imbalance.

You're ready to cut the cord.

In your dominant hand you hold a bright golden sword.

This sword represents your desire to be free and your commitment to peace.

When you're ready, lower the sword and swiftly cut the cord.

The sword effortlessly slices through the cord and you watch the cord fall to the ground.

Take a deep breath in, and on the exhale send out a powerful sigh of relief.

The cord now begins to dissolve into the ground. As it disappears, all remnants of its energy lift off you.

You see this person standing before you.

See them in their innocence.

See them in their light.

Release them.

Breathe in.

Breathe out.

Breathe in.

Breathe out.

When you're ready, open your eyes to the room.

Upon opening your eyes, pick up your notebook and begin to write about your experience.

Take note of how this meditation made you feel. Freewrite in your journal for five minutes.

Pay attention to how you feel throughout the day. Use your journal and take detailed notes. The following morning, you will be ready for your second practice.

Day 2

The meditation for Day 2 is the Meditation for Forgiveness. My hope is that you feel immense relief from this meditation and that you call on it whenever you're caught in the judgment cycle.

The beauty of a spiritual meditation practice is that you don't have to figure anything out. All that is required is your willingness to forgive. Be willing to release your resentment and judgment through your desire to forgive.

Remember that forgiveness isn't something you do, it's a miracle you receive. Follow my guidance and allow this meditation to set the experience of forgiveness in motion. In the final step of the Judgment Detox, we will dive deep into the practice of forgiveness. This meditation will prepare you for what's to come.

Day 2 Morning Meditation: Meditation for Forgiveness

Sit comfortably on a chair or cross-legged on the floor.
Open your notebook, and at the top of the page, write
    these words: I'm willing to forgive.
Then gently close your eyes and prepare for your
    meditation.
Take a deep breath in.
And release your breath.
Continue to breathe long and deep in through your
    nose and out through your mouth.
Breathe in.
Breathe out.
When you're ready, invite in the image of the person
    whom you have judged.
Once again see them standing before you.

*They're brighter now. You feel less attached. The cord
     has been cut and you're already feeling relief.*
*See them standing before you and honor their
     presence.*
Honor their innocence.
Honor their struggle.
Honor their light.
Breathe in.
Breathe out.
*Gently repeat this mantra to yourself as you breathe
     long and deep:*
I choose to forgive you.
I see you in light.
I choose to forgive you.
I see you in light.
I forgive you.
I see you in light.
I forgive you.
I see you in light.
*Repeat these affirmations over and over until you begin
     to feel relief.*
*If your thoughts detour into negativity or mind
     wandering, simply return to your mantra.*
I forgive you.
I see you in light.

*Continue to repeat your mantra silently to yourself.
Whenever you're ready, take a deep breath and open
your eyes to the room.*

When you come out of your meditation, pick up your notebook and free-write about your experience. Don't edit anything. Just let your pen flow for five minutes or more. Trust the guidance that comes through the pen onto the page. Through meditation you connect to your inner wisdom, and the loving voice of your inner guide will lead you toward forgiveness and relief. Remember, this is spiritual healing. You don't have to figure anything out—just let your inner wisdom guide you. Let your love shine through your words onto the page.

You may be surprised by what you write. Don't question it. Trust that your willingness to forgive is enough to let spirit intervene on your behalf. The presence of spirit will guide your thoughts back to love through the healing intention of forgiveness. It's possible that what you write may not be loving at all. Maybe after meditating, you feel even angrier or more upset or resentful. Whatever comes out is absolutely perfect and a big step in your healing process. Let the words flow and don't judge them.

Note any shifts in your thoughts or energy by jotting them down in your journal. Pay attention to how you feel throughout the day. Do you feel lighter, happier, or relieved? Notice how you feel toward the person you have chosen to forgive and how you interact with others.

Be mindful not to judge your process. If you still feel strong anger, resentment, or hurt even after these first two days of meditation, that's fine. There's no right or wrong reaction to meditation. Trust in the process and stick around for the miracles.

Day 3

When we carry a judgment, we are suppressing unfelt rage and anger. I began to notice this when I would meditate to release judgment. I would focus on my breath or a mantra and would begin to relax into my meditation. Then within minutes I'd return to negative, judgmental thoughts. It was almost like I was addicted to them. These thoughts made me emotionally and physically uncomfortable, so I'd try to push them down. I'd forcefully return to my breath or my mantra to avoid feeling the discomfort of the thought. While this helped a little in the moment, I never ended the meditation feeling relieved. Instead I felt even more agitated.

One morning while meditating, I had reconnected to my breath and focused my attention inward. Like clockwork, a judgmental thought surfaced, and my entire focus, energy, and emotions redirected onto that thought. I could feel my energy weaken and my breath shorten. Frustration, rage, and anger began bubbling up. In the moment when frustration hit an all-time high, I received a spiritual intervention. A vision came to me. I saw myself as a young child diving into waves in the ocean. I remember my father teaching me that if you resist the wave, you will get knocked down. But if you dive into the wave you can come out the other side. I loved diving into waves—it was like a beautiful dance with the ocean. In a sea of water that I couldn't control, I could go straight into it and feel free. This image led me to another thought: What if I just dive into the emotion instead of re-sisting it? I followed this idea and began to breathe deeply into the wave of emotion. On the inhale I visualized myself diving into the wave. I'd breathe in and feel all the emo-tion, and on the exhale I'd come out the other side. Within moments I began to feel relieved. I felt free now that I no longer had to push down my emotions or control them. I could simply breathe into the feelings and dive in fully and completely. I spent twenty minutes diving into my emotions and coming out on the other side. No longer judging my emotions, I could simply breathe through them. This prac-tice changed my relationship to my anger forever. I learned that through honoring my rage, I could always come out on the other side.

I named this practice the Meditation for Riding the Waves of Emotion. It's perfect for healing the pattern of judgment because it helps us honor the feelings that live beneath the attack. These feelings may have nothing to do with the judgment at all. It's likely that you've been using your judgment to anesthetize these feelings, since focusing your energy on judgment becomes a way of distracting yourself from the discomfort of unhealed pain. The simplest way to clear the judgment is to dive into the feeling and come out on the other side.

On the third day of your meditation practice, follow my guidance and ride the waves of your emotions.

Day 3 Morning Meditation: The Meditation for Riding the Waves of Emotion

Sit comfortably cross-legged on the floor or upright in a chair.

Roll your shoulders back and gently close your eyes.

Take a deep breath in.

As you inhale, honor all the feelings that are coming up for you.

On the exhale, release the feelings.

Take another deep breath in.

*On the inhale, honor all the feelings that are coming
up for you.*

On the exhale, release.

Breathe in.

And honor all the feelings that are coming up for you.

On the exhale, release.

*Continue this cycle of breath throughout your
meditation.*

Begin to visualize yourself in a crystal blue ocean.

The water is warm and soothing.

No one else is around.

*As you look out onto the ocean, you see a series of
waves rolling toward you.*

These waves represent your emotions.

*You have the power to dive into the waves of your
emotions now.*

You don't have to run from them or be knocked down.

Simply dive into the first wave now.

*As each wave builds height above you, take a deep
breath in and feel all your emotions.*

On the exhale, dive into the wave.

Breathe into each wave of emotion and dive in fully.

On the exhale, come out the other side.

Breathe in and dive.

Breathe out and come through to the other side.

You begin to dance with the emotional ocean of waves
    that continue rolling toward you.

As each new wave approaches it's smaller than the last.

Each wave you dive into becomes easier and easier.

With each breath you feel more and more relief.

In time the waves begin to slow down and get smaller.

With each breath it becomes easier to dive in.

The interval between waves begins to lengthen.

In that time you take long, slow breaths.

You begin to relax into your body.

Soon the ocean becomes still.

You can relax and breathe.

Breathe long and deep and relax into the calm ocean.

You feel a gentle breeze on your face as you lie back
    and float on the water.

Floating in a sea of serenity.

You are calm. You are at peace.

Take one last deep breath in.

When you're ready, open your eyes to the room.

I hope this practice brings you as much joy and serenity as it has brought me. I turn to this meditation whenever I get sucked into the judgment cycle. Honoring your feelings will set you free from the need to judge. It will ease your anxiety and unconscious anger as it brings in a presence of stillness and relief. When you're at peace, there's no negativity to project out. You may find that this meditation becomes a regular practice that you turn to daily to cleanse your energy and release emotional stress.

Day 4

The fourth morning meditation, the Mantra Meditation, will bring you closer to your truth and rearrange your habits. It can improve your concentration and bring calm to even the most scattered mind. In this meditation you'll use the Kundalini mantra *Sat Nam*, which translates as "Truth is my name." Mantra-based meditations can gently guide your thoughts away from the ego chatter and back to a peaceful state.

When you meditate with a mantra, you have the opportunity to experience a transcendent state of relaxation. In this state you lower your cortisol levels and reorganize your nervous system, and when you regularly practice meditating with the mantra *Sat Nam*, you have the capacity to change old habits.

The mantra itself has healing properties. The word *Sat* (pronounced "saht") brings your thoughts to an elevated state and reaches your consciousness toward the spiritual realm.

The word *Nam* (pronounced "nahm") brings that higher consciousness into your bodily experience. When you chant the mantra *Sat Nam* you're calling on the truth of spirit to enter into the physical experiences you're having. Aligning with this truth brings more light into your physical awareness and helps you identify more closely with the love of who you are.

Even with a mantra you'll still notice your thoughts sneak in as you meditate. That's fine. Just witness the thought and gently return to the mantra. If a lot of thoughts come up throughout your practice, that's not a bad thing. It's called an active meditation. The thoughts may not seem to have any relevance to your judgment, but they're showing up in your meditation because something energetic needs to be released. This practice will have great emotional and physical benefits no matter what happens while you're practicing it. Follow my guidance below when you're ready to begin the meditation for Day 4.

Day 4 Morning Meditation: The Mantra Meditation

Sit comfortably cross-legged on the floor or upright in a chair.

Lightly close your eyes and gently focus on the space between your eyebrows (the third-eye point).

Begin repeating your mantra:

Sat Nam.

Sat Nam.

*Breathe long and deep as you continue to repeat your
mantra.*

Sat Nam.

Sat Nam.

If your thoughts detour, gently return to your mantra.

Sat Nam.

Sat Nam.

*Sit for one to twenty minutes, gently repeating your
mantra.*

*When you complete your meditation, slowly open your
eyes and rest your gaze straight in front of you.*

*Don't pick up your phone or quickly get out of your
meditation. Rest for one to two minutes and allow
your body to reintegrate.*

Shortly after this meditation you may feel very energized. Mantra-based meditations have the power to signifi-
cantly lower your stress levels and make you feel relaxed. If
you practiced for longer than ten minutes, it's likely that you
experienced a lot of relief.

By repeating the mantra *Sat Nam*, you allow yourself
to sink into your connection to your own truth. Following

your meditation, pay attention to how you feel throughout the day. You may be less irritable, more energized, and far less judgmental. When you notice yourself lean into a judgmental thought, simply repeat your mantra, *Sat Nam*, and return home. Once you complete your six-day meditation series you may want to come back to this practice as your primary meditation. It's an easy practice that will help you quiet your busy mind and return to peace.

Day 5

The Mantra Meditation has now prepared you for a greater level of relief. The next practice will bring you closer to a connection to oneness. We all long for oneness in our relationships because deep down we know that we are all the same. We all want to feel connected and happy, and we all detour into judgment.

I shared the Meditation for Oneness in my last book, *The Universe Has Your Back*. Many readers reported that they experienced transformational shifts when they surrendered to oneness through this practice. The feedback was so overwhelming that I included the meditation in this step to help you get closer to the experience of oneness and to support you in clearing judgment.

When you practice this meditation, you will feel more interconnected and return to your true essence.

Day 5 Morning Meditation: Meditation for Oneness

Sit comfortably cross-legged on the floor.
Make a fist with your right hand. Point your index
finger up and place your left hand over the middle
of your chest.

Close your eyes and focus on the third-eye point.
I recommend that you play the song "I Am Thine"
by Jai-Jagdeesh during this meditation. Go to
GabbyBernstein.com/bookresources to access the music.

The mantra is Humee Hum, Tumee Tum, Wahe
    Guru; I am thine, in mine, myself, Wahe Guru.
This meditation celebrates our connection with others
    via our shared connection to the Universe. Humee
    Hum *tunes us into our own consciousness.* Tumee
    Tum *accepts that we are one with the other person's*
    consciousness. Wahe Guru *means that we are both*
    connected to the Universe. Then we chant I am thine,
    in mine *to project our consciousness of our personal*
    self to the infinite self. The word myself *confirms that*
    we are one with the Universe. Finally we celebrate
    this universal connection with Wahe Guru.
Chant with the music for up to eleven minutes.

What I love most about Kundalini yoga and meditation are the mantras—they help me remember my interconnectedness with the Universe. If you've never chanted longer mantras before, I encourage you to try it. I chose this specific Kundalini meditation so that you can have an intimate experience of what it truly feels like to release the walls of separation and realign with oneness in your relationships.

Following this meditation, take out your journal and free-write for five minutes about your experience. Let your pen flow and allow your inner guide to write through you.

Witness the words that appear and celebrate any moments of oneness that may have set in.

Then throughout the day pay attention to the way you feel. Maybe you feel more loving, kind, or compassionate. Maybe you feel more closely connected to people. Witness the effect that this meditation may have on you and be proud of your commitment to see oneness. You'll feel a shift in your inner being after practicing it. Have faith in the power of the mantra and your intention that vibrates behind it. When you chant out loud, you make a statement to the Universe that you are ready to heal. Pay attention to the miracles that arise.

Day 6

The final meditation will help you see the person you've judged as if you're seeing them for the first time. I use this meditation when I need to be reminded of our true oneness and to release the pretenses that I've placed upon someone. We all have a shared essence that is beyond our physical site. Reconnecting to the spiritual essence of another person releases them of the judgments and stories you've placed upon them. You can let them off the hook and in turn free yourself from your own suffering. I call this the Great Rays Meditation.

Day 6 Morning Meditation: Great Rays Meditation

Close your eyes.

Sit up straight in a chair or on the floor with your palms facing upward.

Breathe in.

Breathe out.

Breathe in.

Breathe out.

Continue this cycle of breath as you go deeper and deeper into a state of relaxation.

Hold in your mind the relationship that you have judged.

See the person sitting across from you.

Identify the area in your body where you may be feeling discomfort around this person.

Breathe deeply into that area of your body.

On the exhale, release.

Breathe into the feeling.

Breathe out.

Continue this cycle of breath.

Silently offer up this judgment to the care of your inner guide through prayer: I turn this fear over to my inner guide for transformation. I welcome the guidance.

Breathe in: I see you in light.

Breathe out: I release fear.

Breathe in: I choose love and light.

Breathe out: I accept you.

Breathe in: I welcome in great rays of healing light.

Breathe out: All I see is light.

Continue these mantras and allow your inner guide to lead your thoughts back to love and light.

As you repeat each mantra, begin to see great rays of light pour down your bodies.

With each inhale and each exhale, these great rays of light expand.

In time all you see is light.

Repeat your mantras and call in the light:

Breathe in: I see you in light.

Breathe out: I release fear.

Breathe in: I choose love and light.

Breathe out: I accept you.

Breathe in: I welcome in great rays of healing light.

Breathe out: All I see is light.

Relax into the experience of the light and let it take over your consciousness.

Let the light dissolve your judgment.

The light releases your attack.

The light erases all wrongdoing.

The light returns you to love.

All you see is light.

Sit in stillness and enjoy this experience for as long as you wish.

When you're ready to come out of your meditation, take a deep breath in and release.

Then slowly open your eyes to the room.

Give yourself one to two minutes to reintegrate back into your body.

Allow the feelings from the meditation to move through you.

This meditation has enormous healing capacity. In fact, it can change your perception of another person forever. When you see someone in light, you remember who they truly are. This meditation will support your practice of seeing someone for the first time.

At our core we are all light and love. The great rays of light represent our oneness and our true connection. Let this image represent your alignment with the love that is within you. When you see yourself and another in the great rays of light, you have returned to your truest essence.

Following your meditation, take the image of the great rays with you throughout your day. When you think of the person whom you've judged, immediately return to the image of the great rays. When a new judgment arises, close your eyes and imagine your way into the great rays of light.

You may decide to bring this meditation into your daily practice. The more consistently you meditate on the great rays, the easier it will be to call on them for healing. The great rays will become much more than an image. They will represent freedom from judgment and a direct line to love.

Like sunbeams shining down upon you, the great rays are the rays of (nonphysical) light radiating from the presence of love within. We heal our relationship to others and to ourselves by seeing beyond the darkness of our bodies to the rays of light within us all. This meditation aligns you with your true perception, which is nonphysical vision. When you see someone as a nonphysical light, you have chosen spiritual identification and you've remembered that we are all the essence of love. We are not our stories, our dramas, or our wrongdoings. We are love.

Take note of how you feel after this meditation. You may cry with relief; you may sense the energy of love; you may feel forgiveness begin to set in.

I RECOMMEND THAT you not skip any of the meditations in this series. They are designed to build upon one another as you work to release the energetic ties to judgment. Once you've completed the six meditations, choose one to bring into your daily practice.

Even five minutes of meditation in the morning can recalibrate your mind and energy for the rest of the day. Meditation is the way we reconnect to the loving nature within us.

My hope is that meditation becomes an important part of your spiritual practice. Through meditation we slow down our mind and reorganize our energy, which clears space for our inner guidance system to function. But we have to slow down to tune in. The ego will resist meditation, but remember that whatever the ego resists is actually what your spirit needs. The more you make meditation a daily habit, the weaker the ego's resistance will become. You'll grow to rely on meditation to feel connected to love.

This series of meditations has prepared you for Step 6 in the Judgment Detox. In this final step, you'll turn over your experience to spirit more completely and allow spiritual healing to set in. Be open and willing to let love enter into your mind. Step 6 is the most passive and yet the most powerful in the Judgment Detox. Get ready for a sense of completion and freedom in this next practice.

Bring Your Shadows to Light

Early in my journey of personal growth and spiritual development, I became a student of *A Course in Miracles*. The *Course* is a spiritual text on how to undo fear and remember love through the practice of forgiveness. While the text can be intimidating to the new spiritual student (it's long, and a lot of the lexicon is unfamiliar), I realized quickly that its message is profoundly simple: Witness your fear, offer it to your inner guide for healing, and let forgiveness lead to miracles. I was overjoyed by how effective this practice was, and I experienced beautiful shifts as a result of the *Course's* teachings. What resonated with me most, I believe, was the emphasis on forgiveness. I began trying to apply it in all my relationships.

While the lessons in the *Course* are relatively simple, the actual application can be tricky. For instance, it's easy to suggest that someone forgive their boss for not giving them a raise or forgive their roommate for being messy. But how could someone forgive a terrible and traumatic act?

I was particularly challenged to commit to my understanding of forgiveness when I would get questions from my audience members about how they could possible forgive someone who had done something truly horrific—for instance, the person who raped them or the drunk driver who killed their child. Frankly, I was perplexed about how to respond to these kinds of tragic stories.

Overwhelmed by this dilemma, I returned to the *Course* for guidance. This time I was ready to truly know the meaning of forgiveness and let the *Course*'s message sink in. (I found that each time I revisited a lesson in the *Course* I saw it with new eyes, and this time was no different.) I came to understand that true forgiveness requires our willingness to see light in the darkness and replace sin with love. When we are unwilling to forgive, our mind is closed and protects the perception of guilt at all costs.

The *Course* says:

An unforgiving thought does many things. In frantic action it pursues its goal, twisting and overturning what it sees as interfering with its chosen path. Distortion is its purpose, and the means by which it would accomplish it as well. It sets about its furious attempts to smash reality, without concern for anything that would appear to pose a contradiction to its point of view.

Forgiveness, on the other hand, is still, and quietly does nothing. It offends no aspect of reality, nor seeks to twist it to appearances it likes. It merely looks, and waits, and judges not. **He who would not forgive must judge, for he must justify his failure to forgive.** *But he who would forgive himself must learn to welcome truth exactly as it is.*

Our unwillingness to forgive (even the most horrific events) is what keeps us in the judgment cycle. We judge others because we believe that it's a way to protect ourselves from the events of the past. Then we judge ourselves for judging. In the case of deeply traumatic events, we may feel more justified in our judgment of the perpetrator, but that judgment still blocks us from peace. It keeps the traumatic wounds open as we continue to perceive ourselves as victims. Liberation from judgment requires our willingness to forgive. Without forgiveness we continue to live in the shadows of our past and our projections of the future.

This isn't to say we need to forgive immediately. We simply need to be willing to forgive. Our willingness is enough to open the door to forgiveness. When we become willing, spirit hears our call and guides our path. The *Course* says, "Do nothing, then, and let forgiveness show you what to do." Looking at our separation and judgment through the lens of our internal teacher makes forgiveness possible. Spirit will guide us to see that what we perceive others to have done to us is what we continue to do to ourselves. We keep fear alive through our unwillingness to forgive. The moment we become willing, spirit can step in and reverse the effects of judgment and fear.

I went back to my audiences and taught forgiveness with this greater understanding. I invited people to become willing to feel free, willing to release the victim story, and willing to feel happier and safe. Ultimately, forgiving others frees *us* from the burden of judging them. By being willing to forgive—even if we aren't sure how it will happen or how long it will take—we allow ourselves to begin to heal. Forgiving doesn't mean you let someone off the hook for seriously hurting you, and it certainly doesn't mean you need to have this person in your life. But you don't have to expend energy on judging them. You can instead be free. There were no doubters when I suggested the availability of this freedom. Their desire to be free far outweighed their resistance to forgiveness. And because all I asked of them was their willingness, they felt confident and safe in beginning the process. They embraced the truth that forgiveness isn't something we have to figure out or work to accomplish. Forgiveness is a gift that can be bestowed upon anyone who truly wants it.

You find forgiveness by looking at the ego through the eyes of your inner guide. When you witness your ego through this lens of love, you can see the world with more gentleness and patience. Looking at our judgment without attack, guilt, and fear is the essence of forgiveness.

Your willingness to forgive brings the darkness of your illusions to the light of your truth. When you decide to expose your fear to spirit for healing, you are undoing denial and judgment. When you hold tightly to your judgment, you keep it in the dark corners of your mind, where it can never be undone. Living in the darkness leads to resistance and struggle. When you let light shine in, you allow for true healing.

The Judgment Detox concludes with the final step of forgiveness. Steps 1 through 5 have helped you become more compassionate toward yourself and others. Witnessing your judgment and honoring your wounds gave you freedom to begin the healing process. Turning over your judgment to the care of your inner guide through prayer began to open the door for spiritual guidance. The practice of seeing for the first time taught you the true meaning of compassion. And meditation has become your transformational tool for restoring your faith in oneness. To complete the process, we call on forgiveness to fully set you free.

The steps to forgiveness are simple, but your ego will resist the simplicity by trying to convince you that forgiveness is actually far from reach. When this resistance arises, laugh at the ego's mad ideas and accept that you don't have to reach at all. There is no effort here other than your willingness to forgive and your desire for everlasting joy. Follow the guidance outlined below and surrender to forgiveness.

THE PATH TO FORGIVENESS

The workbook for *A Course in Miracles* says:

> *You are not trapped in the world you see, because its cause can be changed. This change requires, first, that the cause be identified and then [second] let go, so*

that [third] it can be replaced. The first two steps in this process require your cooperation. The final one does not.

Forgiveness consists of three steps that guide our judgment back to love.

Set aside your resistance, follow this guidance, and witness the miracles. Be supported by all the work and learning you have done so far. And when you notice your ego arise in this last step, return to your willingness to be free and joyful. Remember that your willingness is all that's required.

The first step in forgiveness is to expose your ego. You do this by bringing your wrong-minded choices to your awareness. Which choices are your wrong-minded ones? Any instances in which you've judged someone else or yourself. You now know that whatever you've judged in another person you've also judged in yourself. However, your ego works continuously to convince you that some outside force is the source of your dilemma, rather than your inward-facing turmoil. As a result, we make idols of people, create special relationships, play the victim, and future-trip by listening to the ego tell us about the problems outside of us. Instead, we must learn to accept that our ego-minded self judges and that our spirit-minded self loves. It's our job to question the ego's thought system so we can understand that we don't have to judge and attack—we need only change our perception of the world.

Whenever you notice yourself go into a place of judgment, the practice is simply to pivot. The moment you witness yourself react with ego and judge, stop yourself and gently expose your ego to your inner guide. When you train your mind to expose your ego it becomes easier and easier to start thinking with spirit. A great *Course* teacher named David Hoffmeister teaches that when the darkness comes up for you, instead of having a harsh reaction, you can actively welcome it. When you seem to be going through something and the ego is judging and reacting, you'll feel like you want to back off and hide. David suggests you allow the ego illusion even when it's terrifying. No matter what it feels like, be willing to bring it to the light. The ego will do everything in its power to justify it. And sometimes your ego's arguments will be convincing. But the pathway to forgiveness is to expose your ego's illusions to the light.

The second step is to accept that you've chosen wrongly and choose again. We must look at our judgment as a projection of our own perceived guilt, sin, and suffering. And we must see that the pattern of placing our suffering outward is a choice we are making. Choosing to be the victim of the world and protecting our pain is how we wound up in the judgment cycle. But behind the veil of guilt and sin is love, which we can experience only when we choose it. The *Course* says, "I have chosen wrongly about myself and now I wish to choose again. This time I choose with the Holy Spirit, and let Him make the decision of guiltlessness for me."

This is an empowering step. Witness the fearful choices you've made and choose to see with spiritual sight. Decide for yourself that you will no longer tolerate the ego's illusions. As *A Course in Miracles* puts it, "No longer be tolerant of mind wandering."

The third step is to ask for help. Specifically, you ask spirit to do for you what you cannot do for yourself. Suspend your ego's beliefs and accept spiritual healing. Spiritual healing is spiritual surrender. By surrendering your desire to forgive and turning it over to spirit for guidance, you let love shine through your consciousness. Be willing to allow spirit to join your mind with the power of love.

Willingness to allow spirit to join your mind with the power of love is all that's needed. Your part in this step is to offer spirit your willingness to remove fear, judgment, and attack, and replace them with forgiveness.

This step is supported by a beautiful prayer from *A Course in Miracles*. You can recite this prayer whenever you are out of alignment with the thoughts of love and are willing to forgive:

> *I must have decided wrongly, because I am not at peace.*
> *I made the decision myself, but I can also decide otherwise.*
> *I want to decide otherwise, because I want to be at peace.*
> *I do not feel guilty, because the Holy Spirit will undo all the consequences of my wrong decision if I will let Him.*
> *I choose to let Him, by allowing Him to decide for God for me.*

When we become willing to invest in love, spirit can step in. Spirit won't take from us what we're not willing to give away. But when we're willing to forgive, spirit can take away our shame, guilt, and sin and help us see love instead.

When you arrive at this point, you've chosen happiness over judgment and love over fear. You are ready to live with more grace and accept that a life of peace and joy is the only sane choice.

When you surrender your judgments to spirit and welcome forgiveness, beautiful synchronicity begins to present itself. You may receive an email out of the blue from the person you've judged—or maybe you even bump into them on the street! Sometimes spiritual forgiveness can come through in meditative stillness, as when I was intuitively guided to send my friend love through my meditation and came out of it to see a text from him. Through that meditation I was able to shift energetically and release my resentment.

Forgiveness comes in unexpected ways. As you practice these steps, stay patient and faithful that relief is on the way. Your inner being is longing to align with love, and the moment you ask spirit for help, that alignment is set into motion. Just relax and know that your desire to forgive is enough and that spirit will show you the way.

Of course, forgiveness doesn't mean you roll over and stay silent about injustice. Spirit may guide you to speak up for yourself as part of your practice. In many cases you will be guided to send a letter to someone explaining your experience while at the same time accepting them for who they are.

Forgiveness also doesn't mean you have to stick around. You can forgive your husband for his abuse but absolutely not stay in the marriage. Remember, forgiveness is a blessing for *you*. When you let go, you release yourself of the tension and trauma that keeps you stuck in a low-level vibration. By releasing that tension, you free your energy field to create a new and miraculous life.

To recap this process, you can apply these three steps silently and swiftly whenever you notice yourself detour into fear:

1. Expose the ego and see your part in the projection of guilt and sin onto others.
2. Be willing to choose again.
3. Invite spirit to enter into your mind through forgiveness.

Remember what the *Course* says:

You are not trapped in the world you see, because its cause can be changed. This change requires, first, that the cause be identified and then [second] let go, so that [third] it can be replaced. The first two steps in this process require your cooperation. The final one does not.

I hope that accepting the simplicity of forgiveness offers you significant relief. Can you now understand that there really is no "application" at all? All you need to do is be willing to see love and let spirit show you the way.

It's time for you to begin to practice forgiveness. Revisit your notes from Step 1 of the Judgment Detox and look at the judgmental grievances you first documented. It's likely that many of them have begun to heal as a result of the previous steps. But forgiveness is still required to allow for full healing. Open your notebook and make three more columns. Put pen to paper and follow this guidance.

In column 1 write down the person whom you've judged and how it has made you feel (remember, this person may be you). Take a close look at the ways the judgment has created more anger, fear, and frustration in your life. In column 2 write about why you're willing to choose again. The final column is where you write your prayer. You can use the prayer from *A Course in Miracles* or make it your own. In writing, offer your judgment over to the care of your inner guide for forgiveness.

Here's an example of what each column can look like:

Step 1: Whom have you judged and how does it make you feel?	Step 2: Choose again and write about why you're willing to let it go.	Step 3: Ask spirit to help you forgive.
I've judged my coworker for making me feel unsupported at work. This judgment has kept me from being happy at my job. I feel angry every day and I can't stop thinking about how I can get revenge against this person. This issue is all-consuming and I take it home with me. It affects my relationship with my family because I am constantly complaining about how upset I am.	I choose to forgive this person so I can feel better. I know that when I let this go, I will have more time for my family, my job, and myself. When I release this resentment, I will also release myself.	Inner guide, thank you for taking this from me. I am willing to surrender this darkness to light and see with love and peace.

Putting pen to paper is a prayer. It's an offering. You humbly look at your judgment, choose again, and then pray for that judgment to be replaced with love. As you practice this step, apply one judgment at a time. I recommend you take this step slowly and pay attention to how it makes you feel over the coming days. In time you'll become so skilled at this step that you often won't even need to write it out—

you'll be able to see the three columns in your mind whenever you're ready to forgive.

Forgiveness is a practice that gets easier with time. Fear has been your habit, but today forgiveness can begin to replace it. Bring this practice to every judgment you have, but I recommend you begin your forgiveness practice with minor, less emotionally charged judgments. Maybe you start with your judgment toward a salesman who ripped you off or the teacher who made you feel inadequate. Give yourself time to practice this step with judgments that feel easy to release. In time you'll become more and more comfortable with this practice, and eventually you'll be able to bring forgiveness to even the most troubling issues.

THE PROMISE OF FORGIVENESS

The promise of forgiveness is freedom from the bondage of judgment and attack. Forgiveness bridges your fear back to love and restores your connection to the love of the Universe. When you welcome forgiveness, you're relinquishing fear and remembering love. Forgiving eyes see only light.

There are many stories of radical forgiveness. One that has stayed with me belongs to a woman named Scarlett

Lewis. I met Scarlett backstage at a talk. At the time we shared a publisher and were on the same speaking lineup. I'd heard of Scarlett's story and her book because of its relationship to the Sandy Hook Elementary School shooting. On December 14, 2012, Scarlett lost her six-year old son, Jesse, when Adam Lanza walked into Sandy Hook Elementary School in Newtown, Connecticut, and killed twenty children and six adults before turning the gun on himself.

After this unimaginable loss, Scarlett looked to hope and faith to heal. She channeled her desire for forgiveness into a transformational book called *Nurturing Healing Love: A Mother's Journey of Hope and Forgiveness*. Even with all the rage, grief, and devastation that came from this tragedy, Scarlett found a way to forgive.

In Scarlett's words:

Forgiveness is central to my resilience. A social worker came to my house shortly after the incident. Kneeling down, with her hand on my knee, she said, "I know how it feels; I've also lost my son and I'm here to tell you the pain will never get better." At that moment I thought, That is absolutely not going to be my journey.

And so I chose the path of forgiveness. Initially

it felt as if the shooter was attached to me by some umbilical cord and all my energy was being sapped. Forgiveness felt like I was given a big pair of scissors to cut the tie and regain my personal power. It started with a choice and then became a process with no neat ending. One day I can forgive and the next I may hear a detail of what happened in the classroom and feel anger all over again.

I also have had to forgive Adam Lanza's mother, who unwittingly armed him and defied medical advice that he should not be isolated. There's a lot of anger for her in the community but I can identify with her because we were both single moms. She paid for her mistakes. He shot her dead before heading for the school.

At Jesse's funeral I urged everyone to choose love rather than hate. I said, "This tragedy started with an angry thought in the shooter's head, which grew to rage and escalated to violence. So please honor Jesse's memory by consciously changing an angry thought into a loving one, to make this a better world." I have come to realize that if Adam Lanza had understood he was more than his thoughts, and if he had received the social and emotional learning support he needed, none of this might have happened. He wasn't born a mass murderer. He had issues at school but instead of helping him, Sandy Hook Elementary passed the problem on to someone else. In this respect Adam Lanza is all our responsibility. Certainly I feel anger at the shooter when I think of the children's fear and what he did to their little bodies, but when I think of the pain that he was in I am able to find compassion too.

I hope Scarlett's story inspires you to find your own scissors and cut the ties of attack. If a grieving mother who lost her child in the most horrific way possible can forgive the person who murdered him, you too can forgive. Let this story empower you to open up to the choice of forgiveness, and let the process begin.

A key part of Scarlett's ability to forgive was her willingness to see Adam Lanza with compassion. She was able to witness his illness and know that he was severely unwell. As you reconnect to spirit through prayer, compassion will become part of your consciousness. Compassion gives you permission to let go. Seeing with compassion helps you understand that people who harm others have been deeply harmed themselves or else lack a fundamental capacity to connect and love, a tragedy in itself.

We all suffer from traumatic wounds. Accepting our collective suffering helps us be more compassionate toward others. It also helps us be more compassionate toward ourselves, and self-compassion is crucial in the forgiveness process. Often the hardest person to forgive is yourself. In some cases people find it fairly easy to let others off the hook, but forgiving themselves seems impossible. When I began to actively practice forgiveness, I noticed I felt a lot of relief in releasing others. But then my ego blindsided me: Just when I began to feel better for forgiving others, my ego redirected my attack back onto me. I started to judge myself for judging others. I attacked myself for my part in each situation and felt unsafe in my forgiveness.

Be conscious of this ego trick. The moment you feel a sense of relief, the ego will show up with reasons why you should attack yourself instead. When this happens, apply the forgiveness steps to yourself. Repairing your connection to your own inner being is essential in healing your perceptions. So when this comes up, look closely at how you judge yourself and how that makes you feel and be ready now to choose again. Your willingness to grow and be happy is what has guided you to get to this point. Trust in this and accept today that you no longer want to be at war with yourself.

Be compassionate toward yourself by honoring all that you've been through. You may find that you're even grateful for your past experiences because they've gotten you to this point. I've found that when I reach moments of relief on my spiritual path, I become grateful for the discomfort I have had in the past. I accept that each experience and ego challenge has been a part of my journey back to love. I forgive my past when I accept that it was part of the journey that got me here. Self-forgiveness requires releasing the past (and staying open to the future) and allows you to live fully in the present moment. In this moment joy can be your choice when you let go of what was and what could be.

Make self-forgiveness a priority by practicing the three steps of forgiveness on yourself. Take a moment to go to your journal to free-write on these topics.

Step 1: How have you been unforgiving toward yourself, and how does it make you feel?	Step 2: Choose again and write about why you're willing to let it go.	Step 3: Ask spirit to help you forgive.

You might be able to think up a number of ways in which you have been unforgiving toward yourself. If so, list them in your rows and offer them up to spirit. The ego will do whatever it takes to judge and attack you to keep you in the cycle of guilt, but the clearest way out of the cycle is through forgiveness. Ultimately, you might find that forgiving yourself is the most profound part of this journey.

On a spiritual level, self-forgiveness is the process of shifting your perception from body identification to spirit identification. When you suspend your bodily perception of yourself and see that you are spirit, you create a miracle moment. This phenomenon is also called seeing with spiritual sight. This type of sight is not visual but internal. You become aligned with your inner being and remember that you are a spirit having a human experience. It's enough if even for a fleeting moment, you see with spiritual sight. These miracle moments are everlasting and bring you closer and closer to truth. The more you practice the principles in this book, the more miracle moments you will receive.

Forgiveness requires practice and repetition. You have to return to forgiveness as often as possible and let the steps become part of who you are. As you practice it, the act of forgiveness will become easier and more joyful. You'll begin to feel less attached to your ego and even laugh at it. When you have enough awareness to witness your ego, you can thank it for another opportunity to practice forgiveness. You'll learn to rely on forgiveness for your happiness and freedom.

Lesson 122 of *A Course in Miracles* guides readers to meditate on this prayer: "Forgiveness offers everything I want."

This lesson reads:

What could you want that forgiveness cannot give? Do you want peace? Forgiveness offers it. Do you want happiness, a quiet mind, a certainty of purpose, and a sense of worth and beauty that transcends the world? Do you want care and safety, and the warmth of sure protection always? Do you want a quietness that cannot be disturbed, a gentleness that never can be hurt, a deep, abiding comfort, and a rest so perfect it can never be upset?

All this forgiveness offers you, and more. It sparkles on your eyes as you awake, and gives you joy with which to meet the day. It soothes your forehead while you sleep, and rests upon your eyelids so you see no dreams of fear and evil, malice and attack. And when you wake again, it offers you another day of happiness and peace. All this forgiveness offers you, and more.

Why would you turn your back on the promise of for-giveness? You've come so far on your journey toward free-dom, and forgiveness is the final step. I know you want to be happy and free. The more conscious you become of the love that exists within you, the more you'll want it. I've found that the more I practice forgiveness, the more I long for it. I can catch myself in a moment of judgment and know in my heart that it's not the choice I want. I can see it clearly for what it is: a wrong-minded choice of the ego. And I can quickly choose again. When the practice of forgiveness becomes a habit, you will begin to truly under-stand the difference between body identification and spirit identification. You'll long to feel the joy of love, and you won't tolerate the ego's terror. Joy will be your choice and spirit will be your guide.

As you come to rely on forgiveness, your life will become more inspired, joyful, and connected. You'll no longer feel at war with the world; instead, you will feel unity and oneness. No matter what goes on outside you, you'll intuitively know to turn inward for what is real. Your inner awareness will become your priority. When this shift occurs on the internal plane, your external experience will be beyond your wildest dreams.

Forgiveness is a constant releasing of resistance. Each time you forgive, you reorient your vision of the world, no longer attached to what you don't want. In this place of non-resistance you can reconnect to your true love nature and be in tune with the vibration of the Universe. You'll feel a palpable sense of expansion, connection, and inner power. In this space of inner connectedness, you'll begin to attract more of what you want because you will no longer be focused on what you don't want.

The way you can stop thinking about something is to start thinking about something else. When you redirect your focus from negativity and resentment to forgiveness, you change your vibration. In the absence of resistance you will become a magnet for what you desire and will feel the energy of love supporting you in every aspect of your life. In this space you'll feel free, present, and alive! You'll begin to rely on forgiveness because it will feel so good. Maybe you even find yourself thanking the people you once judged because they offer you an opportunity to practice forgiveness. You'll be able to silently thank them for helping you become more of what you want to be. You can appreciate your forgiveness practice as the swiftest, clearest path to peace and joy.

Abraham-Hicks say, "A belief is a thought you keep thinking." When you begin to think about forgiveness more than judgment, forgiveness becomes what you believe in.

Like any practice, it gets easier the more you do it. And when you repeat the forgiveness steps over and over, you'll begin to feel momentum. An invisible force of energy will take over and you'll feel relief more quickly.

Eventually forgiveness will become second nature. When you commit each day to finding new ways to forgive, life can become very joyful. You can start to perceive your bodily experience as a fun opportunity to get really good at forgiveness. Each day will bring you new chances to practice. And the more you do, the more you'll narrow the gap between judgment and relief.

You can practice forgiveness all the time. Don't save it just for the uncomfortable relationships. Forgive the small stuff too. In fact, the more you forgive every minor ego moment, the more habitual the practice will become. Forgive your coworker for being slow to respond to your email, forgive the obnoxious driver on the highway, forgive the angry person leaving nasty comments on your Facebook feed. Forgive it all!

In the energy of forgiveness, judgment cannot coexist. **Each step of the Judgment Detox has the power to heal you, but forgiveness is the lesson that makes healing everlasting.** This lesson will change you forever. If you choose to commit to forgiveness, you'll perceive your world in a whole new way. You'll see minor annoyances as interesting opportunities to practice forgiveness. And you'll manage tougher, more uncomfortable situations with more grace. You'll know that you can face any issue because you have forgiveness in your spiritual toolbox. You will never feel overwhelmed by life's challenges, but will instead feel excited and grateful to return to love. Each time you return to love, you get closer and closer to remembering who you really are.

We came here with one purpose: to remember love. Through a series of wrong-minded choices, we built up the ego's resistance, which has held us back in the darkness. But this resistance gives us an opportunity to practice forgiveness. Each moment we choose love over fear through forgiveness is a miracle. Each miracle leads to a greater level of awareness and a deeper connection to love. With practice and repetition, we turn our ego illusions into a miracle mind-set. Living a miracle-minded life allows us to undo fear and return to love. Accept your loving function and get psyched to forgive!

Your forgiveness is not only powerful in your own life, but it also has a ripple effect. Each time you forgive, you create an energetic shift throughout the world. A *Course in Miracles* teaches, "There's only one of us here." On the level of spirit your forgiveness has the power to heal the world. Don't discredit this power. Own it! Accept that you are a miracle worker and each time you forgive you bring more light to the world. As you witness the darkness of the world present itself to you, whether through the news and social media or in our own communities, embrace the darkness and bring in the light. You are the bearer of the light and have great work to do. Let the practice of forgiveness bring a greater sense of purpose to your life. Understand the ripple effect you will have on the world each time you forgive. Your forgiveness will be felt everywhere.

The final chapter of this book will help you apply each step of the Judgment Detox in every corner of your life. As you live the Judgment Detox, you will change the world you see. Nothing will be the same and I can say that with conviction because it happened to me. Using these principles in my day-to-day life has changed me forever. My life has become far happier, lighter, and more abundant in every possible way. Let's make this process fun, enlightening, and energizing so you never turn back! Judgment no longer has to have a hold on you. Love can set you free.

A *Course in Miracles* says, "Love will enter immediately into any mind that truly wants it, but it must want it truly." The steps you've taken in the Judgment Detox have guided you to accept freedom as your natural state of being. Wanting happiness, joy, and freedom is the key to completing these steps. Your desire will keep you on your path and connected to each step along the way. Each time your mind wanders into judgment, ask yourself, "Am I willing to be free?" This question will catapult you back into the practice and the steps will be there to lift you up. Trust this process and know you're always being guided.

As you prepare for the final chapter, take a moment to celebrate how far you've come. The fact that you're on this page of the book reading these words means you made it! Now to complete your journey, I will set you up for a lifetime of freedom with guidance on how to stay consistent with your practices.

I don't want this to be a book you read once, put on the shelf, and forget about. I want the Judgment Detox to become a lifelong practice. My prayer is that you bring these lessons into your circle of family and friends, your community, and your daily consciousness. That's why I dedicated an entire chapter on how to apply these tools in your daily life. This is the moment when you decide whether you will make the Judgment Detox a way of life or something you merely dabbled in. Intuitively I know that you won't choose the path of dabbler. The moments of freedom you've experienced up to this point provide enough momentum to keep you going.

Your desire to be happy is stronger than your ego's resistance. There is so much joy for you in this way of living. Follow my guidance in the last chapter and welcome these steps into your life forever. This is the turning point in your life. Go big and expect miracles!

How to Live the Judgment Detox

As an author and spiritual teacher, I practice what I preach. I hold myself accountable for the lessons I share and always make sure I'm walking my talk. While this is often uncomfortable, because it feels like I'm always working on myself, it's also deeply rewarding. I believe that to teach is to learn. If I'm going to publish spiritual lessons and lecture to audiences, I must wholeheartedly stand behind what I teach. Being a teacher keeps me committed to being a student. Writing this book has been one of my greatest spiritual learning opportunities. I have to fully surrender my judgment and live the steps each and every day.

Throughout the writing process I've felt lighter, happier,

and more joyful. It feels incredible to shift my focus away from judgment and onto love. The freedom I bestow upon others creates a movement of freedom within me. The more I apply these practices, the easier they become. The happiness I've experienced from living this practice is far more valuable than judgment. I've grown to long for the feeling of freedom and am committed to doing whatever it takes to bring more of it into my life.

To top it off, I wasn't the only one holding myself accountable for my judgment. My husband, Zach, has been living the Judgment Detox process with me. Zach has read every page of this book. He's offered edits, wisdom, and advice along the way. Best of all, he's been a mirror for my own practice. Not only has our marriage offered me great opportunities to practice the steps, but he's also called me out when I've fallen back into judgmental patterns. We'd be sitting at dinner and I'd start to rant about someone who'd pissed me off. Zach would shout, "Judgment Detox!" I'd laugh and immediately change my words and tone. His focus on the healing path has helped me stay committed.

It's been a commitment that has completely transformed my life. I was terrified to begin this book because I judged myself for my own judgment. But the moment I started the practice, transformational healing unfolded. I'd find myself with judgmental friends, yet able to remain silent in the midst of their gossip. I witnessed myself refraining from unnecessary social media banter and simply forgive and delete. I've even learned to let myself off the hook and release self-judgment quickly.

Through the Judgment Detox I've received many miracles. I rekindled a friendship that I thought I'd lost due to judgment. I forgave a business associate whom I'd been judging for months. A judgmental story I had on repeat for nearly a year miraculously subsided. I also noticed many physical changes. I began to sleep better. I have far more energy and my immune system became stronger—I was able to stay healthy throughout the winter flu season. Even my eating habits changed! For years I struggled with eating too fast. This was an addiction that I just couldn't kick. Through my practice of releasing judgment I've no longer felt anxious at mealtime. I'm able to taste my food, breathe, and be present throughout each meal.

The most exciting miracle of all is that I'm happier than I've ever been in my life. After surrendering to the Judgment Detox I'm lighthearted, childlike, and free. Best of all, I'm proud of how I'm showing up in the world. It feels good to be silent in the midst of gossip and at peace in the middle of a heated political debate. It's empowering to forgive myself quickly and move forward with ease. It feels great to be a presence of love in the world.

Throughout this process I've taken ownership of my thoughts, words, beliefs, and energy. I've chosen to be a positive force of energy rather than pollute the world with my negative vibes. When I feel powerless over all of the fear and turmoil going on throughout the world, I remember where my true power lies. I return to the power of my loving thoughts and energy and accept that my love is the greatest contribution I can make.

By this point I expect that you've received many of your own miracles. Maybe you've forgiven a family member or maybe you've changed your attitude toward your boss. You've come so far on the path of personal growth and spiritual development. But don't stop now! There's so much more healing and freedom within these steps. My prayer is that this process becomes a part of your daily life—that without even thinking, you default to Step 1 and witness your judgment. And when judgment has you in a headlock, you turn to tapping for relief. Or when you feel separate and alone, you practice seeing for the first time. I hope that prayer and meditation become part of your daily spiritual routine and that forgiveness is your goal in all relationships. When you make these practices your way of life, then you *live a life of miracles.*

GO EASY ON YOURSELF

Now that you've been through all six steps, you can bring more freedom into your practice. You've detoxed and now it's about staying in the flow. Go easy on yourself. Focus on progress rather than perfection. When you notice yourself revert back into judgment (it will happen over and over again!), choose again. You can laugh at the ego's mad ideas, you can forgive the thought, and you can choose one of your steps to return to love.

Don't stress about the steps! The practices in this book can be used anytime, anywhere. You may find one or two steps come more easily to you than others. That's fine! Do what works and don't judge your process. Any one of these steps has the power to heal your perceptions.

Once you've completed the six-step detox at least once, you can then make your own rules. You may find that you spend a month just focusing on your prayers and then get to a place where you feel ready to welcome more meditation. Or maybe you practice EFT for a few weeks and then feel ready to practice seeing for the first time. Do what feels good to you. When you've experienced the complete detox, there's no right or wrong way to continue to apply these principles in your life. All that I suggest is that you use at least one step daily to stay consistent on your path.

My spiritual practice has been built upon freedom, not rigidity. I've loved using steps and methods to help clear resistance, and then once I complete the path, I feel relief. In the space of nonresistance I move forward at my own pace with freedom and ease. Many people make their spiritual practices rigid, but this is just another form of judgment. When we try to be perfect spiritual students, we're actually judging our practice. Now that you've been through all six steps, you can let go of the plan, relax into a place of ease, and gently apply one step a day to stay committed to your loving flow.

FOCUS ON YOUR COMEBACK RATE

You don't have to expect to be free of judgment all the time. Know that you will judge and merely hold yourself accountable for how quickly you return to love. Be less concerned about how perfectly you apply these methods and more focused on how quickly you witness the judgment and come back to your right mind. *A Course in Miracles* says, "You're much too tolerant of mind wandering." Now that you're more aware of your judgmental thoughts, your tolerance for them will decrease. You may even feel fed up with your judgments. That's a good thing! The more aware you are of your judgment, the faster you can choose again and come back to love.

In my own spiritual practice my main focus is my comeback rate. I'm not surprised when I'm judgmental—I anticipate my ego will sneak up on me, and I know life will throw me daily curveballs. My acceptance of my ego is what helps me see past it.

I know that I won't be flawlessly loving, kind, and spiritual all the time, so I make my primary intention to return to love as quickly as possible. The more I've practiced these steps, the more ingrained they've become in my psyche; they've become habit. So when I witness myself revert back to judgment, I quickly apply a step from the Judgment Detox and choose again. When I'm tempted to judge someone on Facebook, I witness my judgment without judgment and say a prayer. Or when a judgmental story is stuck on repeat in my mind, I'll tap on it and get to the root cause of the shame and wounds that live beneath it. Or whenever I'm tempted to judge myself, I'll forgive the thought and return to love.

I use the steps interchangeably throughout the day and celebrate the miracles! Your practice does not have to be perfect. Just focus on coming back fast.

STAY COMMITTED

There's a common problem that people who have gone through any detox can attest to. Once you've finished it, you feel great and think you're cured. Without even realizing it, you stop your practice and fall back into your old patterns. Over the years that I've been on a spiritual path, I've come to realize that when life gets good, we must commit even more to our practice. When things start to flow, the ego seizes the opportunity to convince you that you don't need that spiritual self-help stuff. The ego will deny your spiritual practice and lure you back into your old patterns of separation and attack. That's why daily commitment and practice are required to live a life filled with love and joy.

A *Course in Miracles* says, "An untrained mind can accomplish nothing." We must accept that in order to truly change our habits and release ourselves from the bondage of judgment we must retrain our minds. The six steps of the Judgment Detox have given you a foundation for a new way of being. But healthier habits cannot form (or stick) without daily repetition of the new behavior. Therefore, stay consistent with your practice by repeating at least one step daily to change your patterns. Like any great change, the more you practice, the greater the results.

FIND SPIRITUAL RUNNING BUDDIES

One awesome way to stay consistent with your practice is to get spiritual running buddies in on it with you! A spiritual running buddy can be someone you meet in a yoga class, a person you know through social media, a lifelong friend, or even a spouse. Anyone willing to support you and receive support as you both venture down your spiritual paths will be perfect. When you practice these principles with your spiritual running buddies, you bring momentum to your practice. When one or more gather in the name of love, miracles arise. The collective consciousness of love elevates your practice and supports your commitment. Maybe you set up a local Judgment Detox book club or even host one online through Google Hangouts. If you have friends and family who are on a spiritual path and want to heal their judgment, invite them along for the ride!

Practicing the Judgment Detox with your spouse or romantic partner will transform your relationship. I've found that working the steps with Zach really helps me stay consistent and accountable. We keep each other on track and supported. We now have the ability to honor each other's wounds and shame. Through meditation, prayer, and forgiveness, we've been able to see each other clearly for the first time. This is the greatest healing we've ever received.

The key to a holy spiritual relationship is to be compassionate and understanding of your partner's shame. When you acknowledge that their defense mechanisms arise from shame, you can forgive them. When you recognize that your judgment of them activates their shame, you can choose to heal your behavior. Bringing these principles to life in a romantic relationship will offer you a whole new way of perceiving your partner. The ego goes wild in romantic relationships, so practicing the Judgment Detox will be incredibly useful in helping you release the ego's special illusions and return to oneness, acceptance, and compassion. The Judgment Detox will bring you and your partner closer than you could imagine.

DON'T JUDGE OTHER PEOPLE'S SPIRITUAL PATHS

Throughout the years of being a spiritual teacher, I've witnessed countless people awaken to their own spiritual faith.

While this has been amazing, I've also noticed a common issue: People tend to compare their practice with those of others or judge others for not being on the same path. This is a big no-no. Don't make your spiritual practice another reason to judge. Let people be who they are and honor their path.

I see this issue pop up often in romantic relationships—people complain that their partner doesn't have the same spiritual faith that they do. This is just another form of judgment. I had this experience many years ago when I was undergoing my 200-hour Kundalini yoga and meditation teacher training. I would come home dressed in white with turban on, flying high from practicing hours of yoga, and all I would want to do was share my experience with my husband. My overzealous nature was a bit too much for him. He wasn't interested in hearing about my sixty-minute meditation or my wild spiritual awakening. His apathy toward my yoga really disappointed me. I brought up the issue with my teacher, Gurmukh. I said, "I'm so disappointed because my husband doesn't want to hear about my yoga experience. He's just not into it and I wish he were." Gurmukh grabbed me by the hand and said, "The moment you walk in the door, take off your turban and shut up!" She went on to explain that my practice doesn't have to be his practice. She suggested that if

I just left him alone he could come to a spiritual faith of his own understanding. She guided me to realize that I didn't have to judge him for not being on my path. All I had to do was follow my own and be the light. Gurmukh was right. Accepting Zach exactly where he was on his own path allowed him to step into a spiritual relationship of his own understanding. Today we have many shared beliefs and practices as a result of my letting him move at his own pace.

That is your work. **Just mind your own business and be the light.** Trust that everyone is on their own spiritual path and their own timeline. Your loved ones may not ever share your beliefs, but that doesn't matter. Stay committed to your faith and the Universe will take care of the rest. Trust that as you get healthier and holier, you will elevate everyone you encounter. Your family, friends, and everyone in your life will benefit from your energetic shift. Stay committed to your own path and spread your light no matter what.

While you spread your light, remember that's not the same as being a pusher. It's very powerful to practice these methods with others, but be sure not to push the ideas onto people who aren't interested. Not everyone is ready to let down their defenses and give up judgment. In fact, most people will resist it. If your close friends and family are not on a spiritual path, don't worry, because there are many places to find spiritual running buddies.

PRACTICE PRESENCE

As judgment subsides, you'll find that you have more calm mental space. Be aware that the ego will resist this. Your new mental clarity and positive emotions will be confusing to the ego. Your resistance will make you want to turn to the news for a quick hit of drama or maybe text a friend to gossip. The way to avoid the ego's resistance is to get present in the moment. When you're present in the moment, you don't have to judge the future or the past. In the present moment you can choose to redirect your focus off judgment and onto what is thriving.

Bring presence into your relationships. Be still and listen to others. Give people your attention and enjoy their company. Let yourself learn from others and be curious. When you're present with people, the pretenses you've placed upon them slip away. This is a really fun practice! The next time you're in a social setting with someone you've judged, shift your focus away from what you're judging and onto curiosity. Instead of making up a story about who you think they are, ask them! Inquire about their life, their interests, and their personal stories. When you get curious about another person, you quickly recognize your similarities and human connection. You can see what makes them light up and what makes them shut down. You can lovingly observe them as an innocent child who only wants exactly what you want: love.

I recently experienced the practice of presence miraculously healing my perception of someone. I was at an event and ran into a woman I'd previously judged. My ego's first response was to turn and walk away. But my higher self guided me to show up with love. Instead of wrapping up the conversation quickly and running off to judge her, I chose to be present. I started asking her questions about how she was doing, how her career transition was going, and what new health trends she was into. Within minutes of engaging with her, I started to see her let down her guard. And so did I. The pretenses I'd placed upon her lifted and she immediately felt my judgment release. Once the energy had lifted, we could connect on an authentic level. It turned out that we had far more in common than I thought. We started talking about our love for hiking, fashion, and cooking. She gave me some great recipe ideas. The moment I chose to be present with her, my judgment dissolved and our true connection came forth. This was a miracle.

Maybe you have a colleague you judge, or a friend of a friend. The next time you're with them, practice being present. Ask them questions about themselves and listen. Let down your guard and they will too. You will be amazed by how great it feels to release separation and quickly establish a connection. You may not have anything in common with this person, but when you inquire about them you'll learn something new, and the less you have in common, the more interesting the encounter can be. Lay down your judgment and let them show you who they truly are. Your vibes speak louder than your words. So the moment you let go of your judgment they will relax and feel safe enough to open up to you. Have fun with this exercise!

BE OPEN TO CREATIVE POSSIBILITIES

Another way to access presence and relinquish judgment is to get creative. In a podcast interview with my friend, best-selling author Lewis Howes, we got to talking about the topic of judgment. Lewis is a very inventive guy who's always putting inspiring content out into the world. In our conversation he said, "It's hard to judge when you're being creative." He went on to share that whenever he's in creation mode, writing a book or interviewing someone for his podcast, all his judgment disappears. When his focus is on what inspires him and his attention is placed upon what he's creating, there's no mental space for judgment.

Lewis is spot-on: Often judgment arises out of boredom. When we feel disconnected from inspiration, we look for ways to occupy our thoughts, and the ego gladly steps in. Eventually we find ourselves back in the pattern of judgment. But whenever we put our focus into creative projects, we align our thoughts with inspiration. As Wayne Dyer always said, "To be inspired is to be in spirit." When we're aligned with spirit, our thoughts are connected to love and there's absolutely no room for judgment. So the next time you notice yourself caught in the judgment cycle, dive into a creative project and let spirit take over. If you spend an hour in creativity you'll come out of the experience feeling lit up and energized. You won't want to mess with your high vibes and won't turn to judgment. The more time you spend in creative practices, the happier you will be.

CELEBRATE THE MIRACLES

Throughout your Judgment Detox journey, I've encouraged you to document your miracles in your journal. Now that you've completed the six steps, I recommend you spend some time really celebrating your miracles! A *Course in Miracles* teaches:

> *There is no order of difficulty in miracles.*
> *One is not "harder" or "bigger" than another.*
> *They are all the same.*
> *All expressions of love are maximal.*

Each miracle moment has made an imprint on your energy field and guided your thoughts back to love. The more miracles you add up, the more miraculous your life becomes. Devote some time now to review your miracle moments and take in the magnitude of what you've created. You are a miracle worker!

Accept that any time you shift your perception from fear to love, you experience a miracle. When you acknowledge how far you've come on this path and how much better you feel, it's really tough to turn back. If you make it a practice to continue celebrating your miracles, you'll stay on course.

Paying attention to your progress will keep you committed to feeling good. It's when you forget how far you have come that you lose sight of your spiritual connection.

Each miracle moment offers you spiritual proof that will keep you consistent on your path. When you review your miracles, you can claim proof of the spiritual guidance that is working on your behalf. You'll become even more committed to the practices in this book, because the miracle moments remind you of the power of love. Continue to add new miracles to your journal and review your miracle moments regularly so that you can stay committed to your faith in spirit and the power of love.

LAUGH AT THE TINY MAD IDEAS

Once you've spent some time reconnecting to the miracle moments, review some of the judgments that you documented in Step 1. How do you feel about them now? Do you see them differently? Are you no longer triggered by them? Or could you possibly even laugh at them? The *Course* suggests that we "laugh at the ego's tiny mad ideas." When you laugh at your judgments, you take away their power. It's likely that with your commitment to this detox you're able to look at many of your former judgments and simply laugh. There's nothing more powerful than laughing at the ego. Laughing takes away its power and instantly reminds you how illusory its perceptions are. You have undergone a mental reconditioning and are now ready to see the world in a whole new way. When the ego pops back up, which it will, simply laugh at its mad ideas. You have many tools in your toolbox now. The moment you laugh at the ego, grab a tool and choose again.

KEEP YOUR SIDE OF THE STREET CLEAN

When you live the Judgment Detox practice, you'll feel less and less comfortable when you gossip or say something negative about someone. The reality is that you *will* slip up, your ego *will* get the best of you, and you'll want to justify your anger at times. Accept that this will happen, but have a plan for how you'll clean it up. It's fine to fall back into old behavior, but try to be aware of it. Notice when you slip up and whenever possible clean it up! For instance, I recently had a situation where I was complaining about an independent contractor and the work that they did for me. I told their boss how upset and disappointed I was in the service I received. After the call I felt justified for a moment and then quickly felt ashamed. I realized that I could have expressed my disappointment with far less judgment and much more compassion. I could have said I was unhappy without getting into all the details. I also felt like I added more negativity to the situation, negativity that could have been avoided. So rather than sit in my discomfort and shame, I picked up the phone and cleaned up my side of the street. I called back and took ownership for some of the issues. While this effort may not have made a difference to the person's boss, it made a difference to me. It made me feel like I was taking care of my actions and cleaning up my judgment.

If you find yourself in an unsettling situation where you've judged, remember that it's never too late to clean it up. You can always take ownership of your judgment and wipe the slate. People will respond to this in different ways, but their response isn't what matters (and you can't control it). **What matters is your commitment to love.** By acknowledging your part in a situation, you take a profound spiritual act toward clearing the energy. When you clean up your energy and intentions, the energy of the situation can be healed.

In some cases you may not feel comfortable picking up the phone or confronting someone. That's fine. You can do this work on an energetic level. You'll intuitively know when it's best to do it in person or through spiritual work. If you choose to clean up your side of the street spiritually, do it through prayer and meditation. Pray to heal the relationship and send love to the other person. By sending love to someone, you can cut that dark energetic cord that connects you. You can bring the issue to your meditation practices and return your energy back to oneness and love.

Never underestimate the power of taking ownership of your judgment and clearing it. In the moments when you judge, even if you feel justified, ask yourself, "Would I rather be right or happy?" The answer is always clear.

GIVE YOURSELF PERMISSION TO LOVE

Undoing judgment and returning to love can be disorienting for your ego. Remember, the ego has kept you in the dark for most of your life. You grew to rely on the darkness as your perception of reality. Now with your Judgment Detox practice, you've established a new reality based on love, which may trigger the parts of you that are still holding on to shame. Our disowned shame keeps us from love and blocks us from being vulnerable. Facing your shame, letting down your guard, and opening up in a whole new way may freak you out on the level of the ego. That's cool. Just be aware of it. The more willing I became to face my shame and judgment, the more I was able to recognize my discomfort. I could see how afraid I was to let down my guard and be seen by others, even by those closest to me. Judgment is the barrier we build up against intimacy. When we drop the wall of judgment, we reunite with our capacity to be vulnerable. While this scares the ego, it makes spirit elated. When you're trusting, faithful, and receptive, you're in alignment with your truth.

Be mindful of how the ego will resist love. The more aware you are of this pattern the easier it will be to laugh at the mad ideas and become vulnerable in the presence of love. Honor your shame and surrender to vulnerability. Your authentic truth is your magnificence. Your willingness to let the world see you in truth is your greatest contribution. When we all get real, the world will heal. Give yourself permission to love.

MAKE FEELING GOOD A PRIORITY

A powerful way to stay committed to your Judgment Detox practices is to commit to feeling good. Before practicing the Judgment Detox, I found it easy to fall into negative stories and feelings that would take over my day or week or even longer. Upon completing the steps, I noticed that I was no longer tolerant of unnecessary negative feelings. I wanted to feel happy, connected, and free.

The *Course* says:

The choice to judge is the cause of our loss of peace, and therefore when we meet ourselves and everyone else without judgment we will experience a release and a sense of peace so deep that it will be beyond anything we could possibly imagine.

I experienced this truth, and in a state of peace I became unwilling to go backward. I had experienced great relief from these steps and became accustomed to feeling good, which reset my threshold for discomfort. I no longer wanted to wallow in my sorrow or complain and justify my judgment. I wanted to feel good! I could see clearly how my good-feeling thoughts and emotions were enhancing my life in every way. Feeling good became my priority.

My commitment to feeling good didn't mean that I avoided negative thoughts or feelings. In fact, it was the opposite. Whenever I noticed myself revert back into my ego's tendencies, I'd practice the steps in the Judgment Detox and quickly return to peace. Committing to joy and happiness doesn't mean you run from fear; it means you honor your fear and use your spiritual practice to realign with love as often as possible. The level of success and flow in your life can be directly correlated with your alignment with love. The more joyful you feel, the more life will support you. It's that simple. Therefore, I made the commitment to myself, my family, and my readers that feeling good was my number one priority. With the six steps of this book I can always return to love, and so can you. Make happiness your choice and lean toward joy with every challenge presented to you. Use these steps interchangeably to work through your discomfort and return to love.

EXPECT MIRACLES

This practice, if followed, promises many miracles. Whenever you follow any spiritual path, you will release your resistance to fear and reconnect to love. In the absence of resistance, you become like a magnet for more greatness. This is your attracting power. When you feel good and align with love, your energy sends out a signal to the Universe. Your energy vibrates the clear message that you are aligned with joy and welcome more of it. When you accept this state of being, the Universe can work on your behalf. You'll think of something you'd like to call into your life and it will appear. Old issues that used to baffle you will no longer show up in your life. Obstacles will naturally resolve themselves quickly. And you'll feel a connection to everything and everyone around you. When you dedicate your life to releasing resistance, you accept the love of who you are. In that state of love you'll feel more united, supported, and aligned with what you desire. Life becomes fun and it flows. Love is your natural inheritance, and the Universe responds effortlessly to it. The vibration of love is so strong that it has the capacity to change your worldview and your entire living experience. Healing your worldview will greatly benefit you and everyone you encounter. You'll no longer feel victimized, alone, and separate. You'll honor your connection to every being. This practice offers you that great connection to oneness and inner power.

When you follow this practice, you'll no longer need to look outside yourself for happiness and self-worth. When you're aligned with the presence of love, you know you are good enough, lovable, and powerful. You remember who you truly are. This is the mission of this book. When more and more people realign with their truth, separation will end. Judgment and attack cannot coexist with love and oneness. Terror and fear cannot survive in the light of awakened beings. When people wake up on a large scale, the world as we know it will shift.

We are living in a time that requires us to wake up. It is our birthright to feel connected, and we're called to return to that truth. We must live this truth in every corner of our lives in order to heal the state of the world. This is why we're here: to go on a journey of unlearning fear and remembering love. When one person remembers their true nature, they light up the world.

ACKNOWLEDGMENTS

There are many people who helped bring this book to life. I would like to acknowledge my partner, my husband, and my best friend, Zach. Thank you, Z, for your commitment to helping a lot of people while having a lot of fun! Deep gratitude goes out to my copy editor and dear friend, Katie Karlson, for continuing to contribute love and expertise to all of my books. Many thanks for my spiritual group, Cybele, Brooke, Tracie, Laura, and Sandrine, for your faith in the *Judgment Detox* process. I wouldn't be able to do this without my amazing team, including Davis, Micco, and Jessica, for holding the space for me to be creative and feel supported every step of the way. A big thanks is owed to my Simon & Schuster editor, Diana Ventimiglia, for being so kind and a joy to work with. Finally, thanks to my literary godmother and publisher, Michele Martin, whom I'm blessed to have on speed dial at any hour of the day!